Strength To Carry On

Messages to Strengthen Your Commitment

By Curry R. Blake

General Overseer
John G. Lake Ministries
and
Dominion Life
International Apostolic Church

Copyright © 2013 by Curry R. Blake
All Rights Reserved

Published by
CHRISTIAN REALITY BOOKS
P.O. Box 742947
Dallas TX 75374
1-888-293-6591

Cover Design by John E. Blake.

Unless otherwise noted, all Scripture quotations are taken from the King James Bible.

This book or parts thereof may not be reproduced in any form without express written permission of Curry Blake.

Printed in the United States of America.

The teachings in this book were taken from Sermons given by Curry R. Blake.

Table of Contents

An Impossible Place 1

Constantly Led 21

Co-Workers With God 83

The Coming Revolution 141

The Secret to Constant Victory 177

You Have A Destiny 199

© 2013 Curry R. Blake – John G. Lake Ministries

STRENGTH TO CARRY ON
Messages to Strengthen Your Commitment

AN IMPOSSIBLE PLACE

At one of the healing services, a woman came in wearing an oxygen mask and bringing the oxygen tank with her. She would walk a couple steps and then stop to breathe until she got to her seat on the front row. When it came time to minister, I called all of the DHTs up and had them minister. They prayed for her, and she had great release, but it wasn't quite what she wanted.

I was wandering around just looking for things to pray for. When I got to her, I noticed that she was about seventy percent done. I asked how she was doing, and she said, "I could use one more touch." I said, "Alright." I took her by the hand, and said, "In the name of Jesus, breathe normal."

She took the mask off, breathing normal. Before the service ended, we had praise, and she got up, dancing and singing. When she left, she was dragging that tank behind her, smiling and waving. God was working.

We have moved into a new realm. We are expecting God to do the unusual.

If you went down to the local Wal-Mart, and if you just happened to run into somebody, you would think, "It was good to see them again," or "That was unusual." You have no idea where that one meeting will take you. Every opportunity you get, you should put something in.

Strength to Carry On

Where are you in Christ? Where are you in your heart? Are you farther along in Christ today than you were yesterday? If you aren't farther along today, then you are backslidden. There is no neutral.

Let me ask you something. If God the Father were standing here today and you looked at Him, would you be able to see or perceive any degree of defeat in Him? Has He ever known defeat? No. He is absolute total victory, and even when it looks like defeat, He turns what was meant for bad into good. He is like that for you.

We have to know He is for us. When He is for us, what can be against us?

I want to minister on an impossible place. My life is good. I have no complaints in my life, and I have prayed for that for years. Prophecies I have been given for years and years are all being fulfilled, and I am on the road constantly. We have momentum in the Spirit, and things are good, but it wasn't always like that. There was a time when my life was an impossible place. We couldn't pay our bills; our car was broken down, etc.

The first time I came to Grand Pass, my windshield wipers didn't work, the passenger door didn't open, it was snowing, and there was no heater. A friend of mine was traveling with me. I had to open the door while he stood out in the cold; freezing. We had to drive slowly, because the faster we drove, the faster the ice packed on the window. We had to roll down the window to clean the windshield while we drove down the road. There was no heat, so when we rolled down the window, we froze. We had to wrap blankets around our legs and pull our shirts up over our noses to keep from freezing our lungs out.

We were invited to come and preach, and we were coming. When we got here, the pastor put us in touch with a guy who looked at our van, and by the time we were finished preaching, they had it all fixed, and he wouldn't take any money for it. He came in, and told us, "Your van is fixed. You have windshield wipers, and you have heat." "We have heat?" We were excited about that. You would have thought that we had just won the lottery or something. It was an impossible place. We had no idea we would get here, and the car would be fixed. We expected to have to do the same thing to get home.

I want to talk about an impossible place, because I know that many people believe they are in an impossible place. They have been given a death sentence by the doctor, and they think it is impossible for them to live.

"How is your marriage working?" "We tried, and it just isn't going to happen." "It is impossible for me to kick this addiction. I have tried and tried, and when I try and fail over and over, it is impossible."

I don't consider myself a preacher. I don't come up with a sermon to give you. I pour out of my heart what I believe God wants me to share with you. I am here to share with you; I am not just preaching to you.

If you are in an impossible place, you are in great company. Every person in the Bible was in an impossible place. Take Hebrews 11, and just work through it. Every one of them was in an impossible place. Why do you think they are in the Hall of Faith? They were in an impossible place.

With man, it is impossible, but with God, all things are possible. Do you think there is an impossible place in God? Do you still think you are in an impossible place? If you do, then you are thinking man's thoughts. I am not like Christian Science or that kind of thing, where they say it doesn't exist and think it is just going to go away, because it isn't.

There is a law of faith, and there is a law of fact.

The law of gravity works 24/7; it never stops working and that is a law of fact. You can look up and see a plane flying over head. If the law of gravity still works, why doesn't that plane come down?

It doesn't come down because of another law called the law of lift. As long as the plane goes fast enough with enough wing space to carry that plane, the law of lift will supersede the law of gravity.

The law of faith supersedes the law of fact.

I am not telling you to ignore the facts. If you do that, you will die. You impose the law of faith onto and above the law of fact. It's gotten so that in certain Christian circles, you can't even say anything, because it is negative. We have these code words. "I don't believe it, but the doctor says so." Just because you say what the doctor says, that doesn't mean you believe it.

The Bible says to confess your faults, one to another. I am not saying go around telling everything to everybody. I am telling

An Impossible Place

you to find people who will grab hold of something for you, that will go to God in faith, and will go after it with the Word of God until the law of fact is superseded by the law of faith.

As I said earlier, "If you are in an impossible place, then you are in great company with everyone in this Book." Look at Moses. He had a great sea in front of him, and behind him was the most powerful army of the day. That army had one goal in mind, and that was to catch Moses, and kill him, and put the Israelites back into bondage. The Israelites looked at him saying, "What are you going to do now, Moses?"

You have to realize that just because you are in an impossible place it is not the time to lose heart. That is not the time to give up, and say, "We are going to die." Most of the time, people look at the problem, and then they look at themselves. When you look at the problem, you might say, "You can beat me, because you are bigger than me." Instead, just say, "I am going to beat you."

The part we don't figure in is God's part. "How can God save us? What is He going to do? How are we going to get out of this? We are backed up against the Red Sea." Nobody had ever thought of parting an ocean before. It wasn't like they could all gather together and believe that the ocean would open up.

They got together, and cried out to God, and Moses got in trouble. Moses cried out to God, and God said, "Why are you crying out to Me?" If that had happened to me and I had the Egyptians on one side and the Red Sea on the other side, I would have said, "What better time is there to cry out to You? I can't think of a better time."

God said, "What is that in your hand?" I am sure that by that time Moses had forgotten that he even had that rod in his hand. Moses said, "This is the rod of authority which You told me to take to Pharaoh." God said, "You stretch out your hand, and you part the Red Sea." He didn't say, "You stretch out your hand, and I will part the Red Sea." Now, we know that God did it, but Moses had to act in His stead to bring it to pass. Somebody had to stand and speak for God.

If you are in a situation where someone has told you that you are going to die, that there is no hope, then that is an impossible situation. Maybe they told you that you would have to live with a situation for the rest of your life. In some cases, that can almost be worse. "The eyes of the Lord roam to and fro throughout the whole earth seeking whom He may show Himself strong." That is what is going on.

When you are in that situation, just know that He is looking for those, "in whom He can show Himself strong." He wants someone who will stand in God's place, and speak for Him, and decree for Him, and begin to say, "Let me tell you what is going to happen. By His stripes I was healed, and if I was, I am. Say what you are going to say. Write up all the paperwork, and please give me a copy, because I am going to live longer than you, doctor."

Take that report to God, and say, "Do You see what the Egyptians are trying to say? They don't respect You. They are trying to say that I have to die, but I respect You, and You say that I am healed. I choose to believe You." Put that beside your Bible, and decide what you are going to believe.

An Impossible Place

I have had people call me and ask me to agree that the doctor's report will come back good. No, I am not going to pray that. I will pray with you and agree that you are healed. I will lay hands on you, and minister the life of God into you, and help get you healed, but I will not pray that the doctor's report will come back good. At some point, you have to decide who you are going to believe.

If the report comes back bad, you are going to say, "I guess I am not healed, yet." No, that is the time to say, "You liar. Let every man be a liar, and let God be true." I am not telling you to ignore it. I am telling you to say, "God, they are still lying on You. We need to get this thing done, so they can see it, because I can see it. I know that when Jesus was hung on that cross, His back was whipped, and I was healed, and I can see it, and they need to see it as well." Then, you just go forward.

Noah was in an impossible place. God said, "I want you to build a boat, and save the world." He didn't do all that good of a job. He only saved eight people. I am sure he tried, and he did the best that he could. I am sure the world was pretty wicked.

How would you like to be told that everybody you get on your boat is who the rest of the world will come from? Wouldn't you try to get more people on your boat? Maybe you wouldn't. Maybe you would try a little genetic engineering and try to figure out how many people you would need.

After Moses died, it all passed on to Joshua. In Joshua 1:1-3, it says,

> 1 Now after the death of Moses the servant of the Lord it came to pass, that the Lord spake unto Joshua the son of Nun, Moses' minister, saying,
>
> 2 Moses my servant is dead; now therefore arise, go over this Jordan, thou, and all this people, unto the land which I do give to them, even to the children of Israel.
>
> 3 Every place that the sole of your foot shall tread upon, that have I given unto you, as I said unto Moses.

God told Joshua, "Moses, My servant, is dead. Now, get up, and everywhere your foot shall tread, you shall possess." Tread is a military term.

The Hebrew word for tread is *dârak* and is pronounced daw-rak'. It means *to tread; by implication to walk; go (over), guide, lead (forth), tread (down).* God was saying to Joshua, "Everywhere you marshal your forces and march in like an army, you can take the land."

God didn't say, "March in like an army, and I will give it to you." He didn't say that. God said, "I have given you the land; now march in there, and take it." We want a miracle. The miracle would have been if Joshua had gone to the city of Jericho and found it empty.

The enemy was chasing him. They wanted to gather up all of those people, the Israelites, and put them back into bondage.

An Impossible Place

He didn't get a miracle. He had to go there and do as God commanded him to do. He had to face them, face to face.

We want a miracle, because we don't want to stand and fight. We want everything instantly. There are miracles, and there is healing. Instant healing falls under the category of miracle. Do you know what a miracle is? A miracle is the fire extinguisher on the wall. A miracle is the medicine you keep in your drawer. A miracle is only to be used in response to an emergency.

God doesn't want you to live from miracle to miracle. He wants your life to be stable and steady, so you don't have the valleys and the ups and downs. That way, when the enemy comes, you can see him, and you can beat him, and keep him on the run.

God doesn't always have to give you a miracle to beat him. As long as you keep marching, the enemy will continue to fall; but if you stop, and say, "This is a big problem, and I am a grasshopper," then you are completely leaving God out of the equation. Many times we are grasshoppers in our own eyes.

Smith Wigglesworth used to say, "I am a thousand times bigger on the inside than I am on the outside." He knew Jesus lived on the inside.

God told Joshua to be strong and of good courage, then he told him to be very strong and very courageous. God told him that four times. If I kept hearing that from God and I was on the other side of a mountain, I would ask God, "What is on the other side of that mountain that I need to be very strong and courageous for?"

Strength to Carry On

You don't have to be strong and courageous when you are sitting on the side of the mountain with a nice breeze, on a pretty, sunny day. It is when you get on the other side, and you see those nations that have their weapons sharpened, waiting for you, that you have to be strong and courageous.

Joshua was in an impossible place. He had to face an army. They had been servants and slaves for over four hundred years. They didn't know how to fight. You don't teach slaves how to fight. They were brick makers. Fighting was a new thing for them. He faced armies without an army, and yet he had to be in the lead, because the generals back then were in the front.

All he had was a group of men that stomped in the mud and made straw bricks. That was not a good army, but he had to trust that God, with him, would win.

As soon as they put their foot in the water, the Jordan split, but they had to put their foot in the water first. I am not prophetically gifted so that I can tell you I know where you are and what you are facing. I know that no matter what you are facing, individually or collectively, you are in an impossible place, because we have an entire kingdom of darkness trying to take us out.

Christians have been fighting the war against terrorism for the last two thousand years. Terrorists travel in small groups, so they can hide and disappear. They will not fight you face to face. Terrorism isn't fought face to face. It is fought through fear, and it is against helpless women and children. They do it on purpose, because that is how they bring terror into peoples' hearts. Didn't I just describe Satan?

An Impossible Place

If you go to St. Jude's Children's Hospital and see what is happening to the children who did nothing to deserve it, you will see the parents crying, asking God, "Why did you take my child?" They haven't been trained. I think, "How can we get the truth of the Gospel to people?"

We have to realize that it is time to stand and fight. We have an enemy. Our kingdom wins. I have read the back of the Book, but we have to fight. We can't win without fighting. He gave you weapons and armor. He gave you His Spirit and His power. Luke 10:19 says,

> 19 Behold, I give unto you power to tread on serpents and scorpions, and over all the power of the enemy: and nothing shall by any means hurt you.

Where are you going to go to get more than He has already given you? He has given us Jesus, and Jesus is everything. The Bible even says it again, "If He gave us Jesus, will He not, with Jesus, give us everything?"

When I was growing up, I watched this cartoon about Felix the cat. He had a bag, and whenever he needed something, he would reach into that bag and pull it out. That is who the Holy Spirit is to you. Don't think that is sacrilegious. I am trying to draw an analogy to show you that God has given you everything you need. You may not see it or feel it, but you can reach into the Spirit of God, and pull out whatever you need, because it is in there.

God does not have to decree your healing. He doesn't have to say, "Okay, I have heard you. You have prayed long enough."

God said one time, "Let there be light," and the next thing He said was, "And, there was light." He only said it one time. He put it into motion, and light is still being.

He said in Isaiah chapter 53, verse 5,

> 5 But he was wounded for our transgressions, he was bruised for our iniquities: the chastisement of our peace was upon him; and with his stripes we are healed.

That was the future. They were looking toward the future. It hadn't happened yet. Matthew 8:16-17 says,

> 16 When the even was come, they brought unto him many that were possessed with devils: and he cast out the spirits with his word, and healed all that were sick:
>
> 17 That it might be fulfilled which was spoken by Esaias the prophet, saying, Himself took our infirmities, and bare our sicknesses.

That is the divine commentary. According to Matthew, that is what Isaiah was saying when he said, "He bore our grief and carried our sorrows." It is our sickness and our diseases that He carried. Go on beyond that, after Jesus died and was raised up again, to 1 Peter 2:24,

> 24 Who his own self bare our sins in his own body on the tree, that we, being dead to sins, should live unto righteousness: by whose stripes ye were healed.

That is past tense. You were healed. Where were you healed? You were healed at the whipping post. At that point, you were healed, so it is past tense. It is done.

An Impossible Place

The Israelites looked forward to the cross, even though they didn't know what they were looking forward to. They knew they were looking forward to something. Here we are looking forward to something that has already happened.

Healing is in the Atonement. I can teach for two days on healing in the Atonement and prove it from a dozen different ways. I can show it to you in Communion. Why do you think we take the bread? Jesus said, "This is my body, which is broken for you." When was His body broken? It was broken at the whipping post. In 1 Corinthians 11:24-27 it says,

24 And when he had given thanks, he brake it, and said, Take, eat: this is my body, which is broken for you: this do in remembrance of me.

25 After the same manner also he took the cup, when he had supped, saying, This cup is the new testament in my blood: this do ye, as oft as ye drink it, in remembrance of me.

26 For as often as ye eat this bread, and drink this cup, ye do shew the Lord's death till he come.

27 Wherefore whosoever shall eat this bread, and drink this cup of the Lord, unworthily, shall be guilty of the body and blood of the Lord.

What does it mean to take it unworthily? It means you take it, not discerning the body of Christ. Notice, it doesn't say you don't discern the blood. He went on to say in verses 28-30,

28 But let a man examine himself, and so let him eat of that bread, and drink of that cup.

29 For he that eateth and drinketh unworthily, eateth and drinketh damnation to himself, not discerning the Lord's body.

30 For this cause many are weak and sickly among you, and many sleep.

Sleep means to die prematurely. When you participate in the Communion and you take the bread, and say, "This is His body," and you don't realize that this is His body, broken for healing, then you are taking it unworthily.

When you take the bread, you say, "This is His body broken for me, and in the name of Jesus, I receive my healing, and I am healed now." Then take the juice which represents the blood. At that point, begin to check yourself out, because healing should already be flowing through your body.

The greatest healing service was the night when the Israelites partook of the Passover Lamb. When they partook of the Passover Lamb, they were healed. They all came out the next day, healed. Can you imagine the startled looks the Egyptians must have had?

If you were an employer and your employees came staggering in for work on Monday, all tired and sick, you would think, "This is what I have to work with." If all of a sudden, on Friday, they came in all healthy and ready to go, what would you think? That is how the Egyptians saw the Israelites the day after the Passover.

An Impossible Place

If you don't believe in healing in the Atonement, why do you eat the bread? If we are going to eat the bread, then we should know why we are eating it. We know what the cup is for.

Another illustration of some in an impossible situation and doing an impossible job were the disciples, after Jesus died and rose from the dead. Jesus came back to find that one had betrayed Him, one had denied Him, and one was doubting. There were so few and yet they had to take the world. What if they had not carried out their job? What if they had not accomplished it?"

We are here today because of those few men. They were faithful. They faced an impossible job. Everyone else was scattered, and they were the only ones left. They were sitting around the table thinking, "How are we going to go around the world and spread the Gospel? How are we going to do that?" All they knew was what Jesus had taught them.

All of a sudden, on the Day of Pentecost, they received what they needed. Imagine Jesus looking at them on the Day of Pentecost, and saying. "Here is what we have, and here is what we have to work with." Do you know what He gave them? He gave them the Holy Spirit.

We have the same thing that Jesus gave them to take the world. He could have manifested anything in them, but He said, "The best thing I can give you is Myself, and no man can stand before you all the days of your life."

Is there anything you couldn't take? If you are in a situation, you are in that situation to beat that situation, not to suffer through it. No army has ever been in battle to give glory to their leader by suffering defeat. They are there to win that battle and to win the war, and keep on going.

If you are going to take your city and take your families, you are going to have to learn to overcome. You have to learn to overcome their negativity. You have to look to God, and believe for your family and your cities to be turned around.

I can show you entire cities that have been transformed by the power of God. Jails were shut down, literally, because there was no crime. Hospitals were shut down, because there was no sickness and those buildings became churches. The produce grew four to five times larger than normal. When they checked the ground, they found the soil had more minerals and oxygen in it, because it was turned over to God. It was God's garden. Whatever God does is done big.

If you are in an impossible situation, I guarantee that you aren't in the situation these eleven were in. They had to take the world. All you have to take is your city. Of course, when you get done with your city, move on to the next one until you take the state. Keep on working.

In 1836, there was a group of 186 men in a mission in San Antonio, Texas that decided to stand up to the second most powerful army in the Western Hemisphere. When the army of Santa Anna came into town, this group of men retreated into the mission, which is probably the best thing they could have done.

About the fourth day, the leader, Colonel Travis, sent out a letter to his men informing them of what they had in cattle, etc.

An Impossible Place

He let them know that they were totally surrounded, and there was no hope. They were willing to die instead of surrendering. Their thoughts were: "We believe that if we do this, we can hold this army off for several more days and make this battle costly for them."

They knew that every day they fought they bought more time for General Sam Houston to gather an army, and fight them, and win independence for Texas. These men were not heroes. They were thugs, farmers, outlaws, and criminals. They had no military training at all, but they knew that every day they held Santa Anna's army off was another day closer to victory.

A young man called me the other day, telling me that his mother-in-law was dying because of a large tumor in her mouth. She couldn't eat and was told she had less than 24 hours left to live. He asked me if I would pray, and I said, "Yes, hand her the phone." I prayed for her and had her give him back the phone. I told him to stand and lay hands on her every time he was around her, and command life.

He called me back two days later and told me that there was no change. I said, "What do you mean there is no change?" He said, "She still can't eat. There is no change." I said, "What did you tell me the first time?" He said, "That she was going to die in 24 hours." I said, "Then there is a change, because it has been 36 hours, and she is still alive. Every day she lives, we prove the doctor and the devil a liar, and we win. The more days we win, the closer we get to total victory. Every day she lives is a change. Let's go with the truth that she is healed by the stripes of Jesus."

He called four days later and told me the same thing. I said, "You have to get her 80 percent healed on the inside before she can look better on the outside. Give it a little time. She didn't get this way overnight." I said, "We are not talking about a miracle. We are talking about healing. She is healing, and the "ing" on the end means there is a process."

We want instant miracles, but many times, it's not miracles of healing. It is that they shall lay hands on the sick, and they shall recover. We don't want to go through the process. I agree that is better, but many times that is not how it is. It doesn't say you will get out of bed, and run around. If that doesn't happen, then you have to stand and fight.

In Judges 3, it says that God left nations to test all of the Israelites who had not experienced any of the wars in Canaan. He did this to teach warfare to the descendants of the Israelites who had not had previous battle experience. These nations were left to test the Israelites to see whether they would obey the Lord's commands, which He had given their ancestors through Moses. We find that in Judges chapter 3, verses 1-2:

> 1 Now these are the nations which the LORD left, to prove Israel by them, even as many of Israel as had not known all the wars of Canaan;
>
> 2 Only that the generations of the children of Israel might know, to teach them war, at the least such as before knew nothing thereof;

I am not telling you that God left you sick so that you can learn to fight. I am saying, "Take advantage of the time and learn to fight so that when you come through it on the other side, you are stronger, and you are more aggressive." The enemy will say, "I do not want to go after that person again, because the last time I got my teeth knocked out." You have to get to that point.

Let's go back to Sam Houston. All of the men in the mission had died, and after 13 days, Sam Houston gathered up his men that remained. He was still running, and it looked like he was trying to retreat. Santa Anna's army was so big that it made him think he was invincible, so he made camp in a wide open field.

At that moment, Sam Houston's army, which was a fifth of the size of Santa Anna's army, totally defeated them in 18 minutes. That was because as Sam Houston went, he gathered men and built his army. It looked like he was retreating, but he was using distance as time to build and gather his army.

Whatever you are going through every day, you live through it. You are gaining ground, and the enemy is losing ground. "It has been a long time, and I am tired." Sure, you are going to get tired. It is called battle fatigue. It will come down to one confrontation and a battle that is going to decide the entire thing in a matter of minutes.

When you come down to that, you know you have run as long as you are going to, and it is time to confront him. The devil is a coward. He will try to hide and back off. God will reveal him and make him surrender, and he will give up all the land he has taken.

The impossible place is a place with man, because with man things are impossible, and as long as you think like a man, you will think like the devil. As long as the devil thinks you are in an impossible place, you will draw the devil into an ambush. He will get lazy and sloppy and will not know what is behind him. The thing he thinks is his strength and advantage will become your advantage, because it will turn to his disadvantage.

Goliath's size was his disadvantage, because he saw David in comparison to himself. He did not see David, with God, in comparison to himself, and because of that, David was able to take him.

Just because something looks bad and looks big, like you can't take it, take note: all they see is the tip of the iceberg, because you have God behind you, and He is a lot bigger.

Strength to Carry On
Messages to Strengthen Your Commitment

CONSTANTLY LED

We are going to start this study by discussing revival. Revival is a topic that is usually more talked about than experienced. We will not give you just some type of dictionary definition. We're going to show you how to become revived. Charles G. Finney said, "There are two types of revivals: man initiated revivals, and God initiated revivals." He made it very clear that both are equally valuable.

We teach revival from a position of dominion and from a position of faith in God. You're going to see, through this teaching, that God's entire purpose was for man to have dominion over the earth. If you want to know where we are supposed to end up, go back and look at the beginning.

He said in Genesis 1:26:

> 26 And God said, Let us make man in our image, after our likeness: and let them have dominion over the fish of the sea, and over the fowl of the air, and over the cattle, and over all the earth, and over every creeping thing that creepeth upon the earth.

God's stated goal was for man to have dominion over the earth. God said, "Let's make man and let him have dominion over the earth, and over everything in the earth," and later on He even says, "…and over everything that God made." That is a really strong statement.

God's desire was not for you to be a robot, a machine with push buttons, or a puppet with strings. He has angels who do His bidding. Regardless of what someone teaches, you should return to Genesis, to the beginning, to see what God's desire is and to see what His plan is for man.

A big problem in the church, as the body of Christ as a whole, rather than a specific group, is that the church teaches various doctrines or topics individually or separately. Hence, the church fails to connect the doctrines or teachings into a common thread. The lack of a common thread leads to actual contradictions between the various doctrines or topics. We, on the other hand, teach that doctrines or topics share common threads or common denominators.

Everything we do, everything we teach, has to have a common thread; a common denominator. That common denominator, basically, is dominion.

Dominion and faith are common denominators; they are connected rather than isolated or unconnected topics. Without faith, it's impossible to please God. What pleases God? It is the fulfilling of His plan, which is for man to have dominion. It takes faith to operate in dominion.

You may say, "This doesn't sound like revival." Nevertheless, you must remember that it's not enough to talk about revival; it's not enough to give you a definition. If we're going to speak about revival, the end result should be that we get revived.

An amazing thing occurs, concerning revival, when John G. Lake Ministries (JGLM) teaches around the world. Regardless of what we teach, we get either one of two responses: people either love us or hate us.

Because we teach revival from a position of dominion and from a position of faith in God, people say the same thing, "This just brings freedom; this brings life. You know I came in here sick; yet I am leaving free and healed. This just brings life. Where has this been?"

I say, "It's been right here in this Bible the whole time. You've been taught not to believe it." All we do is teach the Bible to you. I tell everybody, "Anybody can do what we do." As we teach, we see the results in the lives of the people. Yet, you've been taught not to believe it.

Christians, through their choices, amazingly either do not believe or do not want to believe, five simple words: all, whosoever, whatsoever, any, and nothing. Rarely have I met any Christian who truly believes those five words. God said, "Whatsoever you ask." However, people still may offer some other excuse for not believing. They don't believe "all," "whosoever," or "whatsoever."

People may say, "You don't understand. I've got these problems. I can't go over here, because we can't hold a meeting in a Masonic lodge. It may be the biggest building for holding a large crowd, but we can't hold a meeting there because of the atmosphere."

What people are saying is that they do not believe the word, "nothing." The Bible says, "Nothing" shall by any means hurt you." Nothing can stand against you, because nothing can withstand the power of God. People choose which parts they want to believe.

The God we serve is not one in a thousand gods, numbered three hundred, for example. There is no other god bigger than our God. Our God is the biggest god. He is not just the biggest god of the block, or of the world; our God is the biggest god of the whole universe. Jesus said in John 4:23 and 24, when He was talking to the Samaritan woman,

> 23 But the hour cometh, and now is, when the true worshippers shall worship the Father in spirit and in truth: for the Father seeketh such to worship him.
>
> 24 God is a Spirit: and they that worship him must worship him in spirit and in truth.

"The time is coming, and now is, when those that worship God will worship Him in Spirit and in truth." Most people don't worship in Spirit or in truth. What we call worship is begging, complaining, or asking, but it is not worship. When you worship, you bring something to someone with no thought of getting anything back. That statement should change worship in most churches.

True worship is not begging God for power, or for the Holy Spirit to come. True worship is telling God how awesome He is. You worship by telling God what the Bible says about Him or thanking Him for what He's done in your life.

If we're going to worship, we have to realize that there has to be something fundamentally different in the way we do things; different from the way we've done things in the past. Amen?

The purpose of the Five-Fold Ministry is to produce followers who imitate Jesus, and bring into view, the body of Christ. Ephesians 4:15 says that very thing. The Five-Fold Ministry is to produce those that "grow up into Him in all things."

> 15 But speaking the truth in love, may grow up into him in all things, which is the head, even Christ:

The idea that there is a line between you and Jesus is wrong. You, religion, or the devil may draw that line. God, however, does not draw that line. God has broken down the middle wall barrier between God and man. We must always make sure that we are not denying what the Bible says concerning our relationship with God. Revival has to be taught the same way.

Let's read Genesis chapter 2, verse 15,

> 15 And the LORD God took the man, and put him into the garden of Eden to dress it and to keep it.

"And the Lord God took the man," talking about Adam, "and put him into the Garden of Eden *to dress it and to keep it*." "*To dress and to keep*," means simply, *to guard, protect, subdue, or oversee.*

We have to realize that we're not dealing with a god made with hands. If you made a god with your hands, you would be a pagan. You don't make little gold statues of god. If you made statues of god, you could make your god look like whatever you wanted him to be.

I've been to Thailand and Indonesia. They have some of the ugliest gods that you will ever see. The statues are horrific looking things. They formed those gods. I believe that demons spoke to them and gave them a picture of what to draw or put together, and that god is actually a demon that they worship. I think they were inspired by a demon to make that god.

We call things "god" that are not God. Anything you put first in your life is your god. It could be a car, fishing, your job, money, or anything. Usually, you're trying to make money to make your god; where you put your money is usually what your god is.

You must realize: you didn't create God. He created you, and that's why you haven't seen Him. We don't have a statue of Him, because He's too awesome. No matter what statue you made, it wouldn't do Him justice. If you pin up a stick figure drawn by your child, you do not pin up the figure because it looks like you. You hang the figure because your child made it, and you love your child, but it doesn't look anything like you.

If you could make a representation of Him, it still wouldn't put off that glory and still wouldn't show Him as He is. Psalms chapter 8, verse 1 speaks of His glory:

> 1 O LORD our Lord, how excellent is thy name in all the earth! who hast set thy glory above the heavens.

The Bible says that when the people wanted to stone Jesus, He asked them, "Why?" In John 10:33 we read that they answered by saying,

> 33 … For a good work we stone thee not; but for blasphemy; and because that thou, being a man, makest thyself God.

We read in John 10:34-35 that Jesus then asked them,

> 34 ... Is it not written in your law, I said, Ye are gods?
>
> 35 If he called them gods, unto whom the word of God came, and the scripture cannot be broken;

In other words, they're not wrong.

Some people become confused because He said "god." Our definition of the word "god" isn't necessarily the same as the Bible's definition of god. You have to realize what it means when the Bible talks about gods.

There is one God who is above all. There is no God like Him, yet God made man to have dominion and put him over the earth. Essentially, that means that God made man the *god* of this world. The word "*god*" with a little "g" means *magistrate, or ruler*.

Here is the difference. Generally, when we refer to Jehovah God or God the Father, we are referring to a divine being Who is divine in and of Himself, who needs nothing outside of Himself to exist. If we use the word "god" for man, obviously, we're not talking about a being that is, in and of himself, divine and self existent.

Man requires the life of God in him to exist. We are dependent on God to exist so, in that sense, we are not like God. We always say Father God, God the Father, God the Son, or God the Holy Spirit.

For example, if I say, "The sheriff," I might mean the actual elected sheriff over the county or a deputy sheriff. You wouldn't know; unless, I said, "Deputy sheriff," or "The sheriff." They both have "sheriff" in their title. "The sheriff" is one person.

On the other hand, it might be a deputy sheriff who could be anyone of a group of people, although, the last word on his title is "sheriff." The deputy sheriffs aren't operating in their authority; they're operating in the sheriff's authority. That's one of the things that I try to emphasize when I teach on any subject.

We have been taught that we have authority. Yes and no.

I, Curry Blake, do not have authority; unless, I am hid in Christ. "It's no longer I that live, but Christ who lives in me." Then, I do have authority, but the authority I have is not Curry Blake's authority; it is the authority of Jesus Christ. I don't have a little bit of authority; I have the full authority of heaven.

Whatever authority Jesus has, I have. I have full authority, not just a piece of it, because I am a joint heir with Him. That means that whatever He has, I have. My authority is not in me. Regardless of how good I live or how much I do for God, it does not increase my authority. You can't go beyond ultimate authority, which is what Jesus has.

Let me prove it to you by Matthew 28:18:

> 18 And Jesus came and spake unto them, saying, All power is given unto me in heaven and in earth.

"All *power* in heaven and earth has been given unto me." There's that word "*power*" again. We know that "all *power*," the Greek word for *power,* "*exousia*" means *authority*. Jesus was saying, "All authority in heaven and in earth has been given unto me." This is a fundamental difference between what we teach and what is generally taught.

Remember when I told you that most Christians won't believe the word "all?" I'm going to find out if you believe the word "all." If all power and authority in heaven and in earth has been given unto Jesus, how much power and authority does the devil have? The answer is none. If Jesus has "all," then, there's nothing left over. If any power or authority remained, then He wouldn't have "all."

The devil never has authority. He does have ability, because that's what Luke 10:19 tells us.

Jesus has given us His authority, in His name, and the ability to operate like Him, in His stead, over all the power or ability of the enemy.

If Jesus has all authority and the devil has none, and you are in Him, and it is no longer you that lives, but Christ that lives in you, then the "all" authority that Jesus has, is now exerted through you. Whatever He would ask, you can ask. Whatever He would command, you can command.

Except for Christ being the lamb slain, there is no difference between you and Christ. He made you one with Him; in everything else, you're the same. He that is joined to the Lord is one Spirit with the Lord. Whatever He would say or could say, you can say. Heaven will back you up like it would back Him up.

You might ask, "What does this have to do with revival?" That statement, right there, should have revived you. We have the power and authority given to us through Jesus Christ, and heaven will back us up, like it would back Him up.

Let's go to Genesis chapter 2, starting with verse 16,

> 16 And the LORD God commanded the man, saying, Of every tree of the garden thou mayest freely eat:
>
> 17 But of the tree of the knowledge of good and evil, thou shalt not eat of it: for in the day that thou eatest thereof thou shalt surely die.
>
> 18 And the LORD God said, It is not good that the man should be alone; I will make him an help meet for him
>
> 19 And out of the ground the LORD God formed every beast of the field, and every fowl of the air; and brought them unto Adam to see what he would call them: and whatsoever Adam called every living creature, that was the name thereof.

God made them, then brought them to Adam, and said, "Let's see what Adam is going to call them." In Genesis chapter 2, verse 20 we read,

> 20 And Adam gave names to all cattle, and to the fowl of the air, and to every beast of the field; but for Adam there was not found an help meet for him.

In Genesis 1:26, God said,

> 26 And God said, Let us make man in our image, after our likeness: and let them have dominion over the fish of the sea, and over the fowl of the air, and over the cattle, and over all the earth, and over every creeping thing that creepeth upon the earth.

In other words, He was saying, "Let man have dominion over all the earth, and keep it. Let him have dominion over everything that flies, and swims, and crawls." This is what is so amazing to me: God is so faithful. God said, "I've created this whole world which I'm giving to you, Adam. You are going to keep it, guard it, and take care of it."

Adam's job was to have dominion over it, to have authority, to subdue it, and make it obey him. Adam was God's under-ruler. Adam was the person on sight to accomplish God's will on the earth.

We know, however, that Adam did not become God's under-ruler. Later on, when Satan tempted Jesus, he said, "If you will bow down and worship me, I will give you all these kingdoms of the world, because they were delivered to me."

When were they delivered to Satan? The kingdoms were delivered to Satan in the Garden of Eden. Corinthians says, "Whom the god of this world has blinded their minds." Who is the god of this world? It is Satan. He blinds the minds of people; that is what he does. That is his job.

When did Satan become the god of this world? When Adam delivered this world to Satan, Satan then became god of this world. What that means is that for him to get it, it had to be given to him, because he didn't start out with it. When did the shift change? It was when Adam delivered the world to Satan.

No one can give you a kingship, or give you the crown, or give you position and authority unless they have it to give. It was delivered to Satan from Adam. Just as it was delivered to Satan, Satan would have delivered it to Jesus, if Jesus had just bowed His knee.

If Satan became god of this world by Adam giving it to him, then what was Adam before he gave it away? He was the god of this world. Don't become confused by the word "god" with a lower case "g." It just means somebody who is sent to rule or oversee. It doesn't mean divine. Because of that, I want you to see the position of authority and dominion you have.

You say, "Okay, how does this tie into revival?" Take notice, because it has everything to do with why revival happens. Jesus sent out His disciples to heal the sick, raise the dead, cast out devils, and preach the Gospel. (Matthew 10:8)

First of all, He did that to help people, because He loved them. He wanted to help them, and He wanted to undo the works of the enemy. He did it to destroy the works of the devil (Acts 10:38).

When Jesus' followers do those things, they set people free who then become revived. When people become free and revived, they are filled with joy and begin fulfilling God's purpose by blessing others. That's when freedom comes upon people.

That is when man fulfills his purpose, and he blesses those around him. That's our purpose on this earth.

The Five-Fold Ministry is to produce those who "grow up into Him in all things," as it says in Ephesians 4:15. They will go out into the world, and set people free, and bring great joy, which causes the people to respond. They will then come into the church, the body of Christ.

When people respond with great joy, they will bring that joy into the church, and then revival will just perpetuate itself. Perpetual revival should be when believers walk in dominion, exercise their dominion over the ability of the enemy, destroy his works, and show people the goodness of God. The goodness of God draws them to repentance, and it becomes a cycle.

You now know what position we are coming from. It is the opposite of almost all revival teaching which says, "You're not complete, or you're not finished. God hasn't done enough in you. He may have done something, but not enough."

There is a difference between revival and evangelism.

Evangelism gets people saved the first time. Revival is supposed to be for people who have already been saved and have come to God, who then cool off, calm down, or go to sleep in Christ. I don't mean dead, although, it seems that way sometimes. I'm not talking about having physically died. However, a Christian should never have to be revived.

I'm going to show you the New Testament answer to what we call revival. What we call revival is evangelism that's been adapted to believers. You cannot treat a believer, in any state, the same as you can a sinner; one that is not saved. There is a fundamental difference in that the believer has the life of God in them, and an unbeliever knows nothing about God. The unbeliever has no connection with God; there is no life between them and God.

The Bible says that if you love Him you'll keep His commandments, and if you don't keep His commandments you don't love Him.

I got saved when I was nine years old. If you had asked me when I was young, I would have said that I loved God, but I was backslidden and in sin. Did I love God? Technically, according to the Bible, no.

When I was at my worst, when everybody around me was ready to give up on me, there was one person that didn't. There was a friend of mine that would wait at the front door of the night club and walk me home. He never criticized or pointed out the obvious. He would say, "Curry, you know this is not you. You know this isn't who you are. You know you're just biding time, because you're just not doing what God called you to do. You're frustrated." I was frustrated. He never put me down for it. Even when I was at my worst, when everybody else was just ready to throw in the towel, he'd say, "Come on, Christians don't act this way. This isn't you."

I would try going to sleep at night, and I remember crying out to God, literally, just lying on the bed. Every time, before I'd go to sleep or even during the day sometime, I would just stop, and say, "God, don't forget me. You know I'm not going to be like this all my life. You know I'm coming out of this."

A lot of my problem stemmed from the fact that I didn't want to go to church. I told God, "You know I love you, but I just can't stand your children." I didn't like the people in church, and couldn't figure out how to be a Christian outside of church, because I had a wrong idea of what church was. All I'm saying is, "If you've been born again, you may run, but you can't hide."

I'm not telling you to backslide, but one way to know you're really born again is, if you do backslide, there will still be that thing inside you saying, "I'm not staying like this forever; I'm coming out." That's a good sign that the seed of God still abides in you.

Maybe this story will help someone else, because it's not in my notes; it is not what I was intending to say. The amazing thing here is that when God gives man something, He doesn't take it back. This holds true, all the way through all of our experience; that's what I want to get over to you.

In Genesis, chapter 1, He gives man dominion. In Genesis, chapter 2, He makes all of these animals, and He doesn't forget that He gave man dominion. He says, "Yes! I'm going to make all of these things, and take them to Adam, and see what Adam is going to call them."

God remembered; He didn't overstep the bounds. He didn't say, "Adam, call this one this and that one something else." He didn't do that. He said, "Here, Adam, what do you want to call this one?"

In order to realize what I'm trying to get across to you, you have to think. You have to expand or stretch a little, here or there, to see it. If God gives you dominion, and He wants to overstep those boundaries and take control back from you, then that means He's given you something that you may not be walking in. Just because something is not happening doesn't mean it's not God's will. It just means that you are not doing God's will.

If God had brought these animals to Adam, and said, "Adam, here; name them," Adam could have said, "God, You do it. You're awesome. You're God. Whatever You want to do, You can do. Your sovereignty just rules over everything, so God, whatever You want these animals named, You name them."

Now, would the animals have gotten named? No. Why? It is because God gave the animals to Adam to name. If Adam had given them back to God to name, they would have been stuck in no man's land with nobody taking care of them.

What we have to find out is what God has given us to do, because whatever He's given us, He's not going to do. That's what T.L. Osborn always says. He says, "Two things never to ask God: number one, never ask God to do something He's already done, and number two, never ask God to do what He's told you to do." Now, think about that.

If there are things in Scripture that cover a situation in your life, it's not that you're waiting for God to do it; God's waiting for you to do it. He never said to go out and pray for the sick, or to go out and try to get the sick to believe, and He would heal them. He didn't say that. He said, "You go heal the sick."

That means that when you get there, you don't pray to God to do it. That means that when you get there, Jesus, living in you, does it through you. He works through your commands. You're not commanding Him in the sense that, "You better obey me." It's not like that at all.

We are participating just like Jesus participated in the will of the Father, and everything He did was the will of the Father. When He commanded, He wasn't commanding God to do something. He was commanding that sickness obey Him.

Do you realize that sickness and disease have a life? They do cause death, but they have a life. A germ has life. Even though it's not divine life, it exists, it grows, and it eats; it's a living thing.

We're going to go back to Genesis 1:26,

> 26 And God said, Let us make man in our image, after our likeness: and let them have dominion over the fish of the sea, and over the fowl of the air, and over the cattle, and over all the earth, and over every creeping thing that creepeth upon the earth.

Man had complete dominion. Would there be anything there that man didn't have dominion over? No.

Genesis 1:27-28,

> 27 So God created man in his own image, in the image of God created he him; male and female created he them.
>
> 28 And God blessed them, and God said unto them, Be fruitful, and multiply, and replenish the earth, and subdue it: and have dominion over the fish of the sea, and over the fowl of the air, and over every living thing that moveth upon the earth.

I know that it says, "*God blessed them, and God said*," but what that literally means is, "*God blessed them by saying.*" The blessing was Him saying. When He says it, it comes to pass; that's the blessing. He didn't say, "I bless you, now listen to this." He didn't do that; the blessing was what He said. "And God blessed them, and God said unto them, Be fruitful, and multiply…"

That meant that He wanted many people to also have dominion. "And replenish the earth, and subdue it." Let me give you the New Testament version: "Thy kingdom come, Thy will be done on earth as it is in heaven."

If you want to know God's will for your life, it is really simple. Walk around this earth, and wherever you go, in your daily life, and whatever you see, you look at it and give it the heavenly filter. If something doesn't look just right, fix it. You say, "Is this the way it would be in heaven?" If it isn't, then fix it until it looks like heaven.

A sick body is not going to be in heaven. There is no sickness in heaven. Now, if it is "Thy will be done on earth as it is in heaven," how do we know there is no sickness in heaven? That is because it's not God's will. It say's we'll be healed, and there's going to be no crying, no pain. There will be none of that.

Understand, there is no sickness in heaven; none. "Thy will be done on earth as it is in heaven," so it is God's will for there to be no sickness anywhere. If there's any sickness on earth, it should be eradicated by believers, with dominion, subduing the earth.

God said, "And <u>have dominion</u> over the fish of the sea, and over the fowl of the air, and <u>over every living thing that moves upon the earth</u>." That doesn't mean just what crawls around. It means that man is supposed to have dominion over anything in the realm of the earth that is alive or has movement.

What about disease? This is where people get mixed up, because they say, "Well, diseases are caused by demons, but doctors say they can see the disease germs." Well, don't look at those things like they are two separate things that can't be put together or reconciled. They can be reconciled, because it says right here that we have dominion over every living thing.

You can take a disease, and look at it down to its smallest piece. You have germs, you have viruses, you have bacteria; those are living things. They are contagious. Do you know what that means? *Contagious or infectious* means *it can be transferred from one place to another.*

We are to have dominion over every living thing that moves on the face of the earth. It's not just demons we have authority over. You have authority over germs. You have authority over viruses. You have authority over bacteria. You can command that thing, "Die!" and it will die.

We know John Lake did this while he was in Africa. It's been told that it was the Bubonic Plague that killed so many, but it wasn't. It was actually what they call, "Blackwater Fever," which is also known as malaria. It killed thousands.

When they died, they had the foam in their mouths. They looked at it under a microscope, and the germs were moving; they were alive. Lake had dominion over every living thing, so he held the foam in his hand, and gave it back to them. They looked at it again, and all the germs were dead. They asked, "How do you explain this? How did this happen?" He said, "It is very simple. The law of the Spirit of life in Christ Jesus has made me free from the law of sin and death."

Listen to this, though it might sound strange: the "life" of death cannot live around a Christian who has the law, or operates in the law of the Spirit of life in Christ Jesus.

Dr. Lake used to say that the power of God in the spirit realm operates and is similar to the way electricity works in the natural. Do you know where the purest, cleanest atmosphere is? It is the spilt second after a lightning strike; all of the air around it is ionized. It is absolutely pure, and no disease can live in it.

That's what Dr. Lake used to talk about. He said that the lightning of God would flash through men and destroy sickness and disease. That lightning is the power of God. According to the Bible, the Gospel, the Good News of Jesus Christ, His death, burial and resurrection is the power of God unto salvation, healing, deliverance, and prosperity. You name it; it's all there. It is the power of God unto all men. That power of God is faith.

Until quantum physics came along, people couldn't get all of these things together, because they just didn't get it. Now that quantum physics is starting to be explained and understood, now the Bible can be explained scientifically. Scientific people can understand it. Science is starting to catch up with an understanding of how the power of God works.

In the realm of quantum physics, anything can be anything. Isn't that amazing? In quantum physics, there is no set thing; it's a realm of possibilities. We would say it like this, "All things are possible." That's a quantum physics statement. In other words, nothing is settled in that sense, but anything could be, so all things are possible.

When you start to understand this whole idea of faith (we have a series on faith, a series on anointing, a series on gifts), it is like when you get into quantum physics. They all cease to be individual things. They are all the same.

How does a person get healed? Is it by faith? Yes. Is it by the anointing? Yes. Well, which is it? It is both. Is it by a gift? Yes. Do you see? The Bible says that He upholds all things by the word of His power, not the power of His Word; the word of His power. He has power, and He's holding everything together by one word.

That one word was used when He said, "Light be." I don't want to get into quantum physics with it, but that "light" is what holds everything in the universe together. When you start looking at all of this, all of a sudden, the realm of possibility is basically whatever you believe is what's going to end up happening.

When you are believing God's Word, not only do you just have the word of His power, but now you have all of His power behind you, to bring to bear whatever is necessary to change that situation so that it looks like this Word. It is like a deputy sheriff who has all the power of the sheriff when he is enforcing the law. The sheriff has no more power than the deputy.

Let me explain this to you. There are differences in authority. There's internal authority, and there's external authority. Internal authority is the Five-Fold Ministry. We read about this in Ephesians chapter 4, verses 11 and 12,

> 11 And he gave some, apostles; and some, prophets; and some, evangelists; and some, pastors and teachers;
>
> 12 For the perfecting of the saints, for the work of the ministry, for the edifying of the body of Christ:

In here, you may recognize apostle, prophet, evangelist, pastor, and teacher. You may recognize all of those. Outside in the world, they don't recognize them. That doesn't make a bit of difference whatsoever. Anybody who walks out this door may be an apostle in here, but once they're out that door, they're a Christian out there.

The apostle has no more power than the Christian, because demons don't care. Demons don't obey you because you're an apostle. They obey you because you have the name of Jesus and because you're a believer. Amen? The Five-Fold Ministry is internal authority.

Let's say there was an accident, and for whatever reason, a policeman stands out there as a patrolman. He is a brand new rookie on street duty; no stripes or anything. He's out there stopping cars. The cars stop. Why? It is because civilians see a policeman's uniform, they see the badge and the gun, so they say, "Okay, we will stop."

A police captain may pull up, and he may not stop in the line. He may pull on up and talk to the policeman, and then go on around. Why? It is because his authority supersedes the authority of a patrolman.

The people just see a policeman. They don't care if he's a captain or if he's a patrolman. They just know that a policeman has authority. When that patrolman first got there and saw the civilians, he knew that he had authority over them. He knew that he could tell them to stop, and they would, so he used his authority in that way, but when the patrolman saw the captain drive up, he didn't motion for him to stop. All of a sudden, he started saluting and saying, "Yes sir." Why? It is because he recognized internal authority.

All of the ideas you have, "I'm not this, or I'm not that," just know that you're a believer; that's what counts. As you take on more responsibility for the body of Christ, then that internal authority can all be put together.

All of that goes on, but this is not a seminar on the Five-Fold Ministry, so I am not going to get into that. What I'm trying to get across to you is this: don't think that because you're not somebody, that you can't do it, because you are somebody. Being a believer is what counts.

They came to Jesus, and asked, "What do we have to do so that we can work the works of God?" He said, "If you want to do the works of God, it is simple. Believe on Him whom He has sent."

Do you realize that when you believed on Him that was the last work you ever did? Realizing this will set you free, because, from that point on, you ceased from your works and entered into His rest. Now, He is the one that's working; not you.

I told you this would set you free. Why? It is because it means that you don't have to do it. You just let Him out. It should be that we, as believers, have the life of God emanating from us so that we don't have to lay hands, and when they come into our presence, they get healed.

There are a lot of things out there. There are all kinds of camps and different groups, with this teaching and that teaching. It is especially true, when you see groups that are mixing a lot of teachings together. The reason being is because they've been doing it long enough that their followers have heard it, and they've got to keep coming up with new things to keep their followers. That's usually where it comes from, and that's usually where people get into trouble. That's when they start going off and teaching all kinds of weird stuff.

You need to find the truth in the Word of God, and operate in that. My job is not to maintain a position of authority over you. My job is a like a drill instructor in the military. My job is to train you; get you on the field. If I never see you again, I'll know that if I've done my job right, that you can accomplish whatever needs to be accomplished, and you can overcome any enemy that comes your way. I don't have to see you every week, or you don't have to report to me every week so that I know what you're doing, if I train you right.

If you're in an organization, then we try to stay in contact and find out what's going on, but you not staying in contact doesn't take away your anointing. Because of the way we teach, you should grow in this, and it should continue to grow, and we shouldn't create a dependency of you on us as a Five-Fold Ministry.

Our job is to work ourselves out of a job. We should grow you to where you don't need us anymore, and you start to depend on Jesus, in you, rather than always having to run back to Tulsa, Springfield, Rome, or to whoever you relate to.

These things we are bringing up are all Scripture. I'm not going by some big outline or notes; I'm just reading Scripture to you to show you that you can do this. You can read Scripture, and just say what it says.

Did I convince you that you have dominion over every living thing? Did I convince you that germs and diseases are living things? You have dominion over them, to subdue them, to kill them or whatever it takes until whatever body they are in looks like heaven and not like hell.

Strength to Carry On

Let's read 2 Peter chapter 1, starting in verse 1,

> 1 Simon Peter, a servant and an apostle of Jesus Christ, to them that have obtained like precious faith with us through the righteousness of God and our Saviour Jesus Christ:

Is that you? Have you obtained "like precious faith?" Yes? Okay. Notice that he didn't differentiate between different types of faith. The apostle Peter didn't have a different kind of faith than you have, and yet Peter healed the lame and raised the dead by the same faith. You've got that same faith, so you can do the same thing. Now, on to verse 2:

> 2 Grace and peace be multiplied unto you through the knowledge of God, and of Jesus our Lord,

"Grace and peace be multiplied unto you." How is this done? It is done "through the knowledge of God." If you don't have the knowledge of God, you're not going to have grace and peace multiplied unto you. Grace and peace comes and is multiplied to you by your knowledge of God.

If a person comes to me, and says, "Oh, I've got this thing and that thing going on, and I don't know what to do about this," I would tell them as nicely as I could, "Alright, here's your problem. Your mind has not stayed on Him, because the Bible says, 'He will keep you in perfect peace, whose mind is stayed upon Him.'" You need to realize that perfect peace will be multiplied to you by the knowledge of God, so you have a part to play in this.

Let's read verse 3 of 2 Peter, chapter 1,

> 3 According as his divine power hath given unto us all things that pertain unto life and godliness, through the knowledge of him that hath called us to glory and virtue:

"According as His divine power <u>hath</u>…" Notice the word hath; past tense. It means it has already been done, "given unto us." By saying "us," he is saying those who have obtained like precious faith (you and I).

"All things…" There's that word, "all." Do you believe, "all?" Is there anything that you have not been given? This is not a trick question. Just read the Scripture, "All things that pertain unto life and godliness." What have you received that pertains unto life and godliness?

Would healing pertain unto life and godliness? Yes, because if someone doesn't get it, they may die, so it pertains to life.

Do anointing and gifts pertain to life and godliness? Yes, so all of those things you already have, you don't need to chase.

Take notice of this, and it will tell you how He does it: He has "given us all things that pertain to life and godliness, through the knowledge of Him." Isn't that just like verse 2 said, "Through the knowledge of God?"

Those things have been (past tense) given, but how are they experienced in your life? It is, as verse 3 says, "through the knowledge of Him." You can have something and not know you've got it, and if you don't know you've already got it, you won't walk in it, especially if you've been taught or told,

"You've got to chase it, pursue it; you're not finished." It's amazing, because the Bible says clearly, in Colossians 2:10, "You are complete in Him."

> 10 And ye are complete in him, which is the head of all principality and power:

That doesn't say you are completely in Him. You are, but that's not what it is saying. It is saying, "You are complete in Him." In other words, there's no part of you that's missing.

When a baby is born, the first thing you do is count everything, and make sure everything is there. If the baby has eight fingers, two thumbs, and they've got everything there, then, "Thank God, the baby is complete." Is the baby grown? Are they finished? No, but they are complete; you can be complete but not yet fully grown.

When you were born again, you were born complete in Christ. In other words, He's not going to add anything to you. You were complete in Him, but you're going to grow in your knowledge of how to walk in what He has already completed in you.

Go back to 2 Peter 1:3, where he says,

> 3 According as his divine power hath given unto us all things that pertain unto life and godliness, through the knowledge of him that hath called us to glory and virtue:

Notice that word, "virtue." Verse 4 says,

> 4 Whereby are given unto us exceeding great and precious promises: that by these ye might be partakers of the divine nature, having escaped the corruption that is in the world through lust.

"Whereby are given unto us exceeding great and precious promises." Anytime that word, *exceeding*, is used, it means *beyond comprehension; bigger than your wildest dreams*. It is saying, "That by these," referring to these great and precious promises, "you might be partakers of the divine nature."

How are you going to become a partaker of God's divine nature? It is by these precious promises, through the knowledge, and understanding of what they are, and of what you have, and knowing that you are complete in Him, "Having escaped the corruption that is in the world through lust."

Go to 2 Peter chapter 1, starting with verse 5,

> 5 And beside this, giving all diligence, add to your faith virtue; and to virtue knowledge;

"And besides this, giving all diligence, add to your faith virtue." Now, you're complete, but notice what it says. It is not you asking God to add to your faith. Who is adding to our faith? We are. The responsibility is on us to add to our own faith, "virtue; and to virtue knowledge."

> 6 And to knowledge temperance; and to temperance patience; and to patience godliness;

> 7 And to godliness brotherly kindness; and to brotherly kindness charity.

He wants us to keep adding, "And to knowledge temperance; and to temperance patience; and to patience godliness; And to godliness brotherly kindness; and to brotherly kindness charity." Do you hear all of these things that he says to add? That's what you add.

You do it, not God. You do it. God is finished with you; He has done His work. Everything He's done in you is finished; it's complete. What He does, He does well. What He starts, He finishes. It was finished on the cross, and it got finished in you, when you received Jesus. After that, it became your job. I'm going to show you why it's your job to do this. Let's go back to 2 Peter, chapter 1, starting with verse 8:

> 8 For if these things be in you, and abound, they make you that ye shall neither be barren nor unfruitful in the knowledge of our Lord Jesus Christ.

"For if these things be in you, and abound, they make you…" When you hear this, you might ask, "Why don't things work? Why isn't this happening?" I'm going to give you the answer, right now. He said that if you do these things, and they abound in you, then these things in you, "make you that you should neither be barren nor unfruitful in the knowledge of our Lord Jesus Christ."

If you're having failures, you need to add these things to your life. When you do this, it is the discipline of being a disciple.

> 9 But he that lacketh these things is blind, and cannot see afar off, and hath forgotten that he was purged from his old sins.

What that means is that you are not walking in the new creation. You have forgotten that you were purged, and you keep on going back and begging God to do things for you instead of you adding these things to yourself.

> 10 Wherefore the rather, brethren, give diligence to make your calling and election sure: for if ye do these things, ye shall never fall:

When he said, "Wherefore the rather," he was saying, in other words, to listen instead, rather than do that. "Brethren, give diligence to make your calling and election sure: for if you do these things, you shall never fall."

Do you want to know how not to fall? Is it possible not to fall? He just said right there, "If you do these things you won't fall," so that means if you're not doing these things, you will fall. If we don't add these things to us, we will have a tendency to fall, but if we add these things we shall never fall.

In 2 Timothy, chapter 1, verse 6, Paul was writing to Timothy, and he said,

> 6 Wherefore I put thee in remembrance that thou stir up the gift of God, which is in thee by the putting on of my hands.

He said, "Wherefore I put thee in remembrance." Notice that the word "remembrance" has something to do with the mind.

God gave you a new spirit; you are recreated in the Spirit. Your spirit is perfect and complete in Him. Your spirit needs nothing, so you don't need to add anything to your spirit.

Your job, according to Romans chapter 12, verse 2 is:

> 2 And be not conformed to this world: but be ye transformed by the renewing of your mind, that ye may prove what is that good, and acceptable, and perfect, will of God.

Our total endeavors are in the area of the mind, and our job is to renew the mind, and to the degree that your mind is renewed, your life is transformed. It does not say your life will be transformed by a touch from God. The Bible doesn't say that. It doesn't say your life is going to be transformed by someone laying hands on you. It says that your life will be transformed whenever you renew your mind.

We can bless you, and we can help you. We can give you an event that you can take with you, but if you don't renew your mind, you will lose it, and you will be back in another healing line. Is that simple enough? You have responsibility to begin to renew your mind to the truth of the Word of God, rightly divided and understood. The more you do that, the more your mind is renewed, and the less you'll have to stand in lines.

The devil can only work through the part of your mind that's not renewed. That's the only area he can work in. He can't work in your spirit, because your spirit doesn't belong to him. He tries to cloud or blind the minds of people, because He can only work through their minds. His weapons are carnal; fleshly oriented.

Abraham was strong in faith, not weak in faith, and he considered not his own body. The devil will try to get you by working through your mind, to get you to consider your body and forget, "He is faithful, who promised." Is this simple enough?

We just read in 2 Timothy chapter 1, verse 6, "I put you in remembrance that you stir up the gift of God which is in you." Who stirs up the gift of God? Does it say God does? "Well, I'm just waiting for God to move me. I'm waiting for a leading. I'm waiting for the anointing. I'm waiting for a gift." It doesn't say that at all. It says, "You stir up the gift of God." Paul was saying, "Timothy, I'm reminding you that this doesn't just happen! You stir yourself up! You stir up the gift of God that's in you!" How do you stir it up? It's easy.

Understand that I don't have to preach healing to get healing. All I have to do is preach the Word, and healing will occur. If I preach healing, I will get healing, but if I preach the Word, I'll get healing.

Generally, I don't talk much about finances, but if I came in here and preached a whole session on finances, people would get healed as long as what I said about finances was in line with the Word of God. You will get whatever you preach, but you don't have to preach something to get it. You can preach the Word, and healing will occur.

If I preach on healing, there will be some people that don't need healing, but if I preach the Word it blesses everybody. The sick can get healed, and the depressed can get free. Why? It is because I'm preaching the Word, and the Word is life and health to all their flesh. It doesn't have to be specific. Now, if you get specific, that's what you'll get.

People flock to meetings where there are supernatural manifestations. We're just going to talk about those that are of God, at this point. You can walk in the spirit realm, and things will happen. They will be amazing, supernatural things, and they will be of God. Amen? We've all heard testimonies from different people and of things that have happened, and they were just amazing.

There have been so many celebrity preachers, what you might call rock star preachers, which people have put up on pedestals. They say, "This is the guy," and all kinds of things start happening when they preach. It is because of that, that my job, especially in teaching divine healing, has to show the difference between them and me.

When I teach the DHT, I'm teaching believers to do the works of Jesus, so I go out of my way to emphasize the lack of difference between us; between the people I'm teaching and myself. If I teach from a gift of the Spirit, and I talk about a gift of healing or some supernatural manifestation, or if I've fasted forty days and prayed twenty-three hours a day for weeks, and I say, "This is how I got this power," I know that most believers will never do that. I know that. It's a fact.

When I teach the DHT, I purposely keep it at a level that any person can do at that moment, at their level of Christianity, because I preach the simple truth of the Word of God. It is by grace, and it is not by works. Now, do I want to walk at that level for the rest of my life? No.

I've had lots of experiences. I could tell you some things that are not just healing testimonies. I'm talking about other things that God has done and things that we've been blessed to step into at times. I want to move into those things in a more free level, but if I do that, then I won't be teaching the DHT from the level of a believer.

I have to be very specific to tell you how you can do this. It is not based on some action or work, so I have to differentiate. At the same time, as believers, we should start rising to different levels. When I say levels, I'm not talking about God decreeing levels, but I'm saying you've got to step into things; you've got to begin to stir up the gift that's in you.

Believers can lay hands on the sick and heal the sick without being stirred up, but if you get stirred up, it's better! The DHT is just basic level. Here's how you do it: no feeling, no leading, no being stirred up; nothing. It is just the Word of God, fact, and truth.

That's the way it is, but once you get that to operating, then you can start pushing into other areas. There's a difference between what you minister and how you live your daily life. I'm not trying to differentiate between the two; I'm just trying to say there is a difference there.

When I spend time with God, I love it. The more time I spend, the more I walk in the things of God. I have to say this carefully: "It's like the more time I spend with God, the more I want to be alone with Him."

We look at people like Saint Francis of Assisi and some of the old saints that lived back then. They lived in monasteries and they meditated on the Scriptures, and they prayed. I have heard people say things about how, while they were meditating and praying, somebody would walk in, and they would be levitating off the floor about two or three feet and floating in midair.

John Lake, when he was in South Africa, would talk about people sitting on the front pew. As he was praying, these people would start praying, and he would watch them rise off the chair a foot in the air; unusual things. It comes from spending time with God. You don't have to do those things to have the power of God. Those are just personal experiences.

Our problem is that we've taken those personal experiences and made those the standard or requirement to walk in the power of God. I'm trying to differentiate between the two. You can walk in the power of God at whatever level you are. Why? It is because God loves people, and He'll use you, no matter how messed up you are.

Hopefully, you won't stay messed up. Hopefully, you'll get your mind renewed, and you'll spend more time with God. Don't look at spending time with God to get something from Him, but because you want to.

I don't want my kids to want to spend time with me because I'll buy them things, or to spend time with me because I'll pay for everything. I don't want that. I want a relationship where they want to spend time with me.

Most of the time we spend with God, we're there because we need something. You need to get past that to where you realize, "I don't need anything; I have everything." Isn't that what Paul said? "Having nothing and yet having everything." He said, "Making others rich, yet people consider us poor, but we have everything." He was saying, "I don't lack anything; I don't want anything."

You need to realize that you're not there to get an anointing, not there to get a gift, not there to get blessed. You're just there because you love God, and you want to spend time with God. The interesting thing is, when you walk out of there, all the rest of it comes with you, although you didn't go in there to get it.

If your kid always comes to you with his hand out, then your natural human reaction to it is, "What do you want?" When they don't have their hand out, and they just hang around you, and you talk and you fellowship, then all of a sudden, they start to leave and you find yourself saying, "Do you need any money?" That's the way you think, and because they don't ask, you offer it.

We just read in verse 6 of 2 Timothy, chapter 1, where Paul was talking about the gift of God and stirring it up. In verse 7 it says,

> 7 For God hath not given us the spirit of fear; but of power, and of love, and of a sound mind.

This verse talks about how God has not given us a spirit of fear, but of power, love, and a sound mind. Every time he talks, he talks about the power of God. It goes back to doing something with the mind. For the power of God to flow freely from you, the mind has to be brought into alignment; that's the renewing of the mind. The mind works with the power of God and not against the power of God. Let's go on to the next Scripture. In 2 Peter chapter 3, verse 1, Peter says,

> 1 This second epistle, beloved, I now write unto you; in both which I stir up your pure minds by way of remembrance:

"This second epistle, beloved, I now write unto you." In other words, he was talking about the first epistle and the second, "…in both which I stir up your pure minds." Do you hear that? He's talking about stirring up your pure mind. How is he stirring you up? It is, "By way of remembrance." In other words, "I'm calling to your remembrance."

I'm stirring up your mind, and when I stir up your mind, you're going to go back and do what? You're going to stir up the gift that is in you like Paul told Timothy. He was saying, "I'm stirring up your mind; I'm reminding you."

Remember when you were at that conference, and they laid hands on you? Remember how you felt, and remember what they taught? Your pure minds have to be stirred up by remembrance.

Verse 2 says,

> 2 That ye may be mindful of the words which were spoken before by the holy prophets, and of the commandment of us the apostles of the Lord and Saviour:

Remember, "That you may be mindful of (or think about) the words that were spoken before by the holy prophets, and of the commandment of us the apostles of the Lord and Saviour." He is telling you how you are going to stir up your mind, and that is by thinking about the Word of God.

You need your mind stirred up; you need your spirit stirred up. When your mind and your spirit get stirred up, when you stir up the gift that is in you, and you stir up your mind by remembering the Words of God, and you start putting the Words of God into effect, then your body is going to follow. It is going to go with you as your soul and your spirit are stirred up, together, to get the Word of God done.

In Jude chapter 1, verses 20 and 21, it says,

> 20 But ye, beloved, building up yourselves on your most holy faith, praying in the Holy Ghost,
>
> 21 Keep yourselves in the love of God, looking for the mercy of our Lord Jesus Christ unto eternal life.

He says, "But you, beloved, building up yourselves (that would be like stirring yourself up in a way) on your most holy faith, praying in the Holy Ghost." When you are praying in tongues, it not only stirs you up, but it also builds you up. It strengthens you; it edifies you.

Notice what he puts with this. When you do this, "Praying in the Holy Ghost and building yourself up, you will keep yourselves in the love of God, looking for the mercy of our Lord Jesus Christ unto eternal life." This is how he tells you to keep yourself.

In Ephesians chapter 5, starting with verse 17, it says,

> 17 Wherefore be ye not unwise, but understanding what the will of the Lord is.

"Wherefore be ye not unwise, but understanding (understanding has to do with the mind) what the will of the Lord is." He was saying "If you do not know the will of God, you are unwise." He was saying, "Don't be unwise, but understand what the will of God is."

> 18 And be not drunk with wine, wherein is excess; but be filled with the Spirit;

"Okay, Paul. How do we get filled with the Spirit?"

> 19 Speaking to yourselves in psalms and hymns and spiritual songs, singing and making melody in your heart to the Lord;

These are the things you do to stir yourself up.

You say, "I thought we were going to hear about revival." You are; I'm telling you how to be revived. I'm telling you how to stay revived. I'm telling you how you stay stirred up; how you stay strong. That's the difference.

I don't come to meetings to get pumped up. I stay pumped up, because if I don't stay pumped up, guess what? People die. People call me every day; they call me all hours of the day. I don't have the luxury of "not being revived."

When the Welsh revival happened in 1904, they asked William Booth, "Are you going to go up there and visit?" He said, "No, I'm not going to go." They said, "Why not? We thought you liked what was going on." He said, "I do. I'm for it, but I can't go up there, because if I do, I'll shut it down."

They said, "Well, why would you shut it down if you like it?" He told them, "No, I'm not going to go up there and shut it down on purpose, but if I went there, my presence there would shut it down, because I am bigger than that revival." You might think, "That was very conceited." No, it was his understanding of who he was in Christ, and to what degree. He realized that and said, "I'm not looking for a move of God; I am a move of God." That's what you need to realize.

The Bible says in Matthew 24:23,

> 23 Then if any man shall say unto you, Lo, here is Christ, or there; believe it not.

Here, Jesus was saying, "When they say 'Lo, Christ is over there,' or 'Lo, Christ is over here,' don't go out there." The word "Christ," makes us think they were saying, "Look, Jesus is over here or over there." There is truth to that, but the word means "anointing" or "the anointed one." When Jesus was saying, "If they are saying, 'Look, the anointed one is over here, the anointed one is over there,' don't run out to them." Why? It is because the Kingdom of God is within you. You don't have to run to an anointing; you don't have to run to this meeting or to that meeting.

Now, when we come together, it's good to fellowship together. We're not against having meetings, but don't think you're going to be lacking something if you don't go. You don't lack anything, because you are complete in Him.

When we do these things and are running here and there, we are violating Scripture if we're going there to try and get something. "Well, I've got to get this anointing. Well, you know he operates in the prophetic, so I've got to go over there so I can operate in the prophetic anointing. Well, you know he operates in visions and dreams, so I've got to go over there to get this anointing for dreams." No, if they're out there doing it, by the Spirit of God, you've got the One they're doing it by.

You may want to go somewhere and hear something taught so that you learn how to walk in it, but don't go there thinking, "Well, I've got to go there to get his hands on me so I can get what he's got." No, no, no, you've already got what he's got.

You can run around for the rest of your life going to meetings, but if you don't start doing what you've been hearing, then you'll spend the rest of your life running to meetings, and honestly, you'll be a hearer of the Word and not a doer. You will be deceived by those that you're running to hear, because they will tell you, "You've got to get this, or you have to have that." No, you don't.

I just told you what God said for you to do. The responsibility is on you to add to your own faith virtue; and to virtue knowledge, etc. You don't get those things by having hands laid on you. You get them by getting the Word of God in you. Remember, we read in verse 19 of Ephesians chapter 5:

> 19 Speaking to yourselves in psalms and hymns and spiritual songs, singing and making melody in your heart to the Lord;

Here he says, "Speak to yourselves in psalms and hymns and spiritual songs." That's how you get stirred up; that's how you get built up; that's how you get strong in Christ.

Let's go to 1 John 5:18,

> 18 We know that whosoever is born of God sinneth not; but he that is begotten of God keepeth himself, and that wicked one toucheth him not.

"We know that whosoever is born of God sinneth not (doesn't make a practice of sin); but he that is begotten of God keepeth himself." Who keeps him? He keeps himself. We know God keeps us, because God will keep whatever we commit to Him, but here it doesn't say God will keep you; it says that you will keep yourself.

The reason I'm doing this is because I want to show you that the emphasis is on us; it's not on God. It's not on you getting down in front of an altar and screaming, begging, and crying until something happens. What you're looking for to happen happened when you got born again, but you've never learned to not walk by feeling. Now, you're trying to get a feeling; some kind of feeling that will give you evidence that you have what you've already got, and you don't need that.

You need to understand what faith is. Faith trusts the Word of God, believes it to be true, and then acts like it is true. Pay attention to this; this is an awesome promise: "We know that whosoever is born of God sinneth not; but he that is begotten of God keepeth himself, and that wicked one toucheth him not." Wouldn't you like to live in a place where the wicked one doesn't ever touch you?

He tells you right there how to do it. "Keep yourself. Be born of God; sin not." You say, "Well, I'm trying not to sin." I'm going to tell you how not to sin. You say, "You mean we can live without sinning?" Yes. You're expected to. That's not some high and lofty thing. You should have known that when you got born again. Notice what it says in Ephesians 6:16:

> 16 Above all, taking the shield of faith, wherewith ye shall be able to quench all the fiery darts of the wicked.

It says, "Above all..." There's the word "all" so that means above everything else; there's nothing else above this. "Above all, taking the shield of faith..." Faith is important, because it says, "Above all." "Wherewith (the shield of faith) you shall be able to quench all (there's the word "all" again) the fiery darts of the wicked."

If above all, you take the shield of faith, with it you can quench (put out), every fiery dart that comes your way. How do you think the wicked one toucheth you not? You're going to put out every fiery dart he throws your way. That means that you can live in a place where the wicked one touches you not, because you keep yourself, and by your shield of faith, the fiery darts never get to you.

If you want to talk about revival, this should bring revival. The devil can't just come into your life. It says, "He goes about seeking whom he may devour." That means he can't devour everybody. Most Christians that I talk to would never say this, but really they believe the devil is just a little below God. They think, "He's the god of this world, so he's equal. He's just a little lower, because you wouldn't want to say anybody's equal. He's right there. He's the next level down." No! He's not!

Let me give you this hint: the devil has you convinced that he's much more powerful than he is, and you have bought that lie. Let me show you how I know this to be true. Remember when Jesus was born? Three wise men came along, and said, "We're looking for this king. The stars show a king has been born." These astrologers, astronomers, whatever you want to call them, were three wise men from the east. They went in to find Jesus, and they found Him. Satan, working through Herod, tried to kill Jesus. He put out a decree that all males, two years and under, should be killed.

Now, think about this: three men found Jesus, and the devil couldn't. The wise men were the smartest. Amen? Think about it. You would think the devil could at least look at the same stars the three wise men did, but you have to understand, his mind is blinded. He is in darkness. The devil couldn't find Jesus, but man could. That gives you an idea that he's not as sharp as everyone thinks he is. He has just convinced you that he is.

If you don't want him to know something, don't tell him! The reason he knows your thoughts is because he put them there, and you speak them out. He doesn't just read your mind, unless your mind is his mind. What I'm trying to get you to realize is that you can live in a place, but it's your responsibility how you live there. I'm trying to show you from 2 Peter 1:10 where it says that you can live in a place of protection.

> 10 Wherefore the rather, brethren, give diligence to make your calling and election sure: for if ye do these things, ye shall never fall:

I am honestly amazed, most of the time, at how protected I am and how God takes care of me. He blesses me in spite of myself; it's amazing! I have favor with God. You have favor with God. I don't have some special favor. Do you understand that? I'm starting to realize that favor and walk in that favor. It's amazing, this blessing of God!

I'm not chasing after the blessing of God. Even under the Old Covenant God said, "If you do these things, blessings will overtake you! It doesn't say for you to chase them. It says that they will chase you. If you chase them, you may get something, but it's really hard.

I want to be effective for the Kingdom of God; that's what I'm after. I want to be as effective as possible. Honestly, there are times where it's almost like, "God, I don't need that blessing; it will slow me down."

God brings you things and blesses you with things. You have to be careful what you ask for, because you'll get it. Have you ever realized that if someone you love mentions something they like, you want to go back and get it for them? God does that. When you walk with Him, and you please Him, and He's pleasing to you, it's amazing!

You'll notice things, and say, "Yeah, I kind of like that." You're not even thinking about it, and a few days later, you'll get it. Somebody will buy it, and give it to you. You should say, "That is pretty, God, but I don't want it." I know it sounds foreign to some people, but I'm telling you, that's the way God is. He's amazing! He will lavish things on you as long as things don't become your god. Amen?

Let's move on to the next Scripture in 1 Corinthians 15:34. Here is the key; this is the main Scripture. I'm going to tell you how not to sin; it is really simple:

> 34 Awake to righteousness, and sin not; for some have not the knowledge of God: I speak this to your shame.

"Awake to righteousness, and sin not." Do you want to know how not to sin? "Awake to righteousness." When you realize that you are the righteousness of God, in Christ, and when your righteousness with God truly becomes real to you, sin just drops away. It loses all of its appeal.

You don't have to have it beaten out of you. "Don't drink; don't smoke!" How many of you know that there are too many sins for you to go down the list, and get them all? It's simple. If you want to know how not to do this, this, and this, and 10,000 other things, "Awake to righteousness." It's not what you don't do; it's what you do. Amen?

"Awake to righteousness, and you will not sin." Isn't that simple? Let me give the definition of *righteousness: to be righteous or made righteous; to be made as one ought to be.* When I read this, it was amazing! When you got born again, God made you what you ought to be. You were complete; it was done. He fixed you; you are what you should be. "Well, you know I'm not perfect yet." No, we're all still renewing our minds, but you are what God made you. If you are in Christ, you are made righteous.

You are not a new evolution. You are a new creation, which means you were created complete and perfect in Him. You're not going to evolve into it.

Your mind, the renewing of your mind, is an evolution. You evolve into understanding, but you were born again, in right standing with God. You're not any more right now than when you got born again.

There are no different degrees of righteousness; you're righteous. Our battle is in renewing the mind, but don't think that you've got to become something. You are what you needed to become. Now, you just need to renew your mind to line up with who you are. When you do that, everything starts working. You start thinking differently, and talking differently. Romans 10:4-8 says:

> 4 For Christ is the end of the law for righteousness to every one that believeth.

5 For Moses describeth the righteousness which is of the law, That the man which doeth those things shall live by them.

6 But the righteousness which is of faith speaketh on this wise, Say not in thine heart, Who shall ascend into heaven? (that is, to bring Christ down from above:)

7 Or, Who shall descend into the deep? (that is, to bring up Christ again from the dead.)

8 But what saith it? The word is nigh thee, even in thy mouth, and in thy heart: that is, the word of faith, which we preach;

It says, "How does righteousness which is by faith speak?" Righteousness, which is by the law, says, "I fasted, I prayed, I paid my tithes; I did everything right, and because of that, I'm right with God." That's righteousness which is by the law. That doesn't work, because no man was made righteous by the law. He said that not knowing that, they went about to establish their own righteousness, trying to do things to get right.

How does righteousness, which is by faith, speak? It doesn't say who will ascend into heaven and bring Him down. It doesn't say who will descend and bring Him up. No, the righteousness, which is by faith, says, "The word is nigh us; it's in our mouth, and in our heart: that is, the word of faith, which we preach (speak)." It is the Word of God. Isn't that simple?

I don't know about you, but in me, this knowledge is just exploding, and I'm saying, "Glory to God! These are exceeding and precious promises!" It doesn't get any better than that. It starts to come alive in you! Come on! Try to get revived! I dare you to stay dead! Read this, and try to stay dead!

You can't stay dead reading this and believing it. Why? It is because, it is life! You know that if you play in mud, you get muddy. If you play in the Word of God, you get righteous; you get faith; the gifts operate. All of this starts working through you.

Remember what it said in 1 Corinthians 15:34,

> 34 Awake to righteousness, and sin not; for some have not the knowledge of God: I speak this to your shame.

"For some have not the knowledge of God." There's that word knowledge, again. Isn't it strange how everything we're supposed to be doing goes back to our knowing something? Why? It is because you are complete. You've got to figure it out. It means that your mind has to line up; you have to renew your mind to the Word of God. If you've been through the DHT, you've already heard me talk about this, so I'm not going to go into detail. It says in Hebrews chapter 5, verses 12 and 13:

> 12 For when for the time ye ought to be teachers, ye have need that one teach you again which be the first principles of the oracles of God; and are become such as have need of milk, and not of strong meat.
>
> 13 For every one that useth milk is unskilful in the word of righteousness: for he is a babe.

It says, "For everyone that uses milk is unskillful in the word of righteousness." When it's talking about the "word of righteousness," it's talking about the Word of God as a whole, but notice it specifically says, "If you have need of milk and not strong meat, it is because you are unskillful in the word of your righteousness and right standing with God."

In other words, until you understand your right standing, until you understand that you have been made right with God, until you understand that you are as you ought to be, then you will always be a babe in Christ and never grow up and take your position. You'll always need milk, and you'll always be unskillful in the Word, because you'll always be trying to get something rather than walk out who you are.

This is what is important: righteousness. The church understanding its rightness with God is the key to everything. Talking about quantum physics and science, the church was looking for the single theory, what they call the unified theory. It is the one theory that explains everything. They used to say it was the string theory. They want this one theory so they can say, "By this one theory, we can understand everything." I'm telling you that if the church will begin to walk in righteousness, it will understand everything.

Righteousness is what the world is looking for. They are looking for their rightness with God. They are looking for that one thing that makes everything else line up.

You can have faith, but if you don't understand righteousness, you won't use your faith. You'll ask God when to use your faith, and you'll always be looking for something. If you have gifts, you'll think, "Should I use it, should I not? How do I use it?" You'll always be looking for things, but once you understand righteousness, then you realize who you are in Christ, how you have been made, who you ought to be, and then you'll understand that you can't use your faith the wrong way.

All of the other people try to tell you how to do things right. All of the other teachings, even on healing, try to tell you how to do things right. If you understand righteousness, you will know that Jesus did not heal the sick because He did everything right. He did everything right because of Who He was with God.

He understood that, and He kept trying to tell them, "I and my Father are one, and We are going to be one." Jesus prayed in John 17:21:

> 21 That they all may be one; as thou, Father, *art* in me, and I in thee, that they also may be one in us: that the world may believe that thou hast sent me.

He is in us, and we are in Him. It's going to be great! We're all going to be one! He said, "You don't get it, and until you get it, you're always going to be trying; you're always going to be struggling." It wasn't that Jesus did everything right, it was that He couldn't do anything wrong.

I've tried to pray so as not to get results. I'm not going to explain to you how or why, but God still answered my prayer, even though I was praying in the way I was taught. He shouldn't have answered that kind of prayer, but He still answered it.

He said, "I'm going to heal them because of your relationship with Me, not because of their relationship with God." That just revolutionized my life. I thought, "Give me Scripture," because I was trying to not get the prayer answered, and God gave me Scripture. He took me back to Abraham, and it said that God spared Lot, because He remembered Abraham.

Let's go back to Hebrews chapter 5, verses 13-14,

> 13 For every one that useth milk is unskilful in the word of righteousness: for he is a babe.
>
> 14 But strong meat belongeth to them that are of full age, even those who by reason of use have their senses exercised to discern both good and evil.

"For everyone that uses milk is unskillful in the word of righteousness for he is a babe, but strong meat belongs to them that are of full age." He goes on to say, "Even those who by reason of use (you're doing something, not to get it, but to experience it, to walk it out) have their senses exercised to discern both good and evil."

Let's go back to Genesis 2:15-17,

> 15 And the Lord God took the man, and put him into the garden of Eden to dress it and to keep it.
>
> 16 And the Lord God commanded the man, saying, Of every tree of the garden thou mayest freely eat:
>
> 17 But of the tree of the knowledge of good and evil, thou shalt not eat of it: for in the day that thou eatest thereof thou shalt surely die.

God gave man two commands: have dominion (subdue the earth), and don't eat of that tree. Basically, those are the only two commands He gave. One command was, "Do," and the other was, "Don't."

Let's go to Matthew chapter 22, verses 35-40,

> 35 Then one of them, which was a lawyer, asked him a question, tempting him, and saying,
>
> 36 Master, which is the great commandment in the law?
>
> 37 Jesus said unto him, Thou shalt love the Lord thy God with all thy heart, and with all thy soul, and with all thy mind.
>
> 38 This is the first and great commandment.
>
> 39 And the second is like unto it, Thou shalt love thy neighbour as thyself.
>
> 40 On these two commandments hang all the law and the prophets.

"Then one of them, who was a lawyer, asked Him a question, tempting Him, and saying, 'Master, which is the great commandment in the law?'" In other words, "Which one do I have to follow?"

"Jesus said unto him, 'Thou shall love the Lord thy God with all thy heart, with all thy soul, and with all thy mind.'" Notice how many times the word "all" is there: "all" thy heart, "all" thy soul, and "all" thy mind. "This is the first and great commandment."

He added a second to it. "And the second is like unto it." In other words, "It is equal to it." "Thou shall love thy neighbor as thyself. On these two commandments hang all the law and the prophets." In other words, "If you do these two, you will fulfill all the law and the prophets."

Notice that God gave Adam two commands: to have dominion (subdue the earth), and don't eat of that tree.

Notice that Jesus said there are two commands that are above everything else: love God with everything you've got, and love your neighbor as yourself.

Jesus gave two commands; both of them positive. With Adam, one was positive and one was negative. "Do," and "Don't do." With Jesus, both of them were positive. "Do," and "Do." In 1 John chapter 2, beginning with verse 3, it says,

> 3 And hereby we do know that we know him, if we keep his commandments.
>
> 4 He that saith, I know him, and keepeth not his commandments, is a liar, and the truth is not in him.

You don't get to know Him by keeping His commandments. Keeping the commandments proves you know Him. You don't do the commandments to try and be right or stay right. If you're right with God, you'll do right. It's an outflow. "He that says, I know Him, and keeps not His commandments is a liar, and the truth is not in him." In verses 5 and 6, it says,

> 5 But whoso keepeth his word, in him verily is the love of God perfected: hereby know we that we are in him.

> 6 He that saith he abideth in him ought himself also so to walk, even as he walked.

That's how the world should even see us. If we say we know Jesus, we ought to walk like Jesus.

In 1 John 3:22-24, it tells us,

> 22 And whatsoever we ask, we receive of him, because we keep his commandments, and do those things that are pleasing in his sight.
>
> 23 And this is his commandment, That we should believe on the name of his Son Jesus Christ, and love one another, as he gave us commandment.
>
> 24 And he that keepeth his commandments dwelleth in him, and he in him. And hereby we know that he abideth in us, by the Spirit which he hath given us.

What does that mean? It means we walk by faith. When we read the first part, where it says, "We keep His commandments," you can't be thinking, "Don't curse, don't steal, and don't smoke." Those aren't His commandments. His commandments are: believe on Him whom He has sent, love Him, and love your neighbor as yourself. Those are the two commandments Jesus gave.

If you love God, and you love your neighbor, you won't steal, because your neighbor owns the things that you would be stealing. You won't covet, right? You won't do that.

The emphasis is on loving God, not on not doing those things. There are a lot of moral people that don't steal and don't curse that are not saved, so not stealing, not cursing, not doing those things doesn't do it. You don't do those things, because you are right with God. "Awake to righteousness, and you will not sin."

The last Scripture is 1 John chapter 5, beginning with verse 1,

> 1 Whosoever believeth that Jesus is the Christ is born of God: and every one that loveth him that begat loveth him also that is begotten of him.
>
> 2 By this we know that we love the children of God, when we love God, and keep his commandments.
>
> 3 For this is the love of God, that we keep his commandments: and his commandments are not grievous.
>
> 4 For whatsoever is born of God overcometh the world: and this is the victory that overcometh the world, even our faith.

"His commandments are not *grievous*," meaning *they are not hard*. "For whatsoever is born of God overcomes the world." Do you hear that? Whatever is born of God overcomes the world; not is overcome by the world. It's not by what you suffer or what you are going through. It is by you overcoming the world. "And this is the victory that overcomes the world, even our faith."

How are you going to overcome? By faith which means what? Not considering what you see; not considering your body. Be strong in faith, giving glory to God knowing that He is faithful, who has promised. You keep walking until the result that you see in the Word is the result that you see in the physical.

In verse 5 of 1 John chapter 5, it says,

> 5 Who is he that overcometh the world, but he that believeth that Jesus is the Son of God?

The whole purpose of this was very simple. It was to show you in a small way who you are in Christ; that you are made right. In that sense, you are revived. Amen? Now, you can shout, jump and run because you're revived. Shouting, jumping and running doesn't mean you're revived; it's a fruit of being revived.

In all of these verses, we were talking about knowing Him and keeping His commandments. It all had to do with how you treat people and how you love God. It had nothing to do with a service, had nothing to do with music, had nothing to do with shouting, and had nothing to do with excited emotions. It had to do with you aligning your soul with the Word of God and doing what He said to do.

As you do these things, do them because you are right; not to be right. Because you are right, you love God and you love your fellow man, and you do unto them as you'd have them do unto you.

What I really want you to understand is that God has done everything He's going to do. Healing is in redemption. He's already done everything He's going to do for you.

He has given us these promises: "By these promises, we become partakers of His divine nature; by these promises He has given us everything that pertains unto life and godliness." Why? He gave us Jesus, and with Jesus, He also gave us all of these other things. It all happened at the new birth.

He also said that you've been blessed with every spiritual blessing in heavenly places, so that's done. All blessing is done; all healing, "By whose stripes you were healed," is done. All of that's done.

God has done everything He's going to do, but He has told you to do some things. Stir up the gift that's in you; stir up your pure minds by remembering the Word of God. He has told you to do these things, and He also said that you need to add to your faith virtue, knowledge, temperance and all of these things.

If you do this, you will never fall. You will keep yourself, and if you keep yourself, the wicked one will not touch you. If he doesn't touch you, you're not going to get sick again. You can live in divine health.

God goes way beyond just healing. He goes way beyond just giving you a blessing. He goes way beyond just feeding you. He will show you how to stay fed; He will show you how to stay healed. He will show you how to walk in life.

If your focus is only on you, all you care about is getting healed, but if you focus on others, your focus will be on staying healed so that the life you have is enough to give away.

I tell people, "One of the biggest lies in the church is that Jesus came to give us an abundant life." That is a total and absolute lie. Jesus did not come to give you an abundant life. The Bible doesn't say that, but it's been misread so many times that we have adopted it. He did not say He came to give you an abundant life.

Drug dealers have an abundant life. They have cars, they have money, they have houses; they have everything. That's an abundant life. Having a life with a lot of things is an abundant life.

Jesus said, "I have come to give you life and that more abundantly." That's something no drug dealer has; no drug dealer has life in abundance. They may have an abundant life, but they don't have life in abundance.

Life in abundance means that I have so much life that it keeps me well, and I even have life in abundance so that I can give away life. I have enough life left over, that not only do I stay well, but I have life left over so that I can get others well, too. That is life in abundance. No drug dealer has that. That's the difference.

That life that's in Him is righteousness. It is faith, and it is gifts. It is everything, because it's all the same. Do I have anointing? Yes. Do I have gifts? Yes. Do I have the Spirit of God? Yes. Do I have power? Yes. Do I have faith? Yes.

You ask, "Which one are you going to use to get me healed?" All of it will be used, because it's all life. Life is faith, life is anointing, and life is gifts. Why? It is because it's divine life. By these precious promises, we become partakers of the divine nature of God, and we have that "Zoë" life. That is life as God has it; that life that just keeps perpetuating itself.

Strength to Carry On

Strength to Carry On
Messages to Strengthen Your Commitment

CO-WORKERS WITH GOD

We were in a place in the United States many years ago, up in the mountains. It took hours and hours to drive there, and there was hardly anything there. There was little housing, and they had a major conference there. There were probably between 4,000 and 5,000 attending.

When they started, they had several other ministers there. I could name them, and you'd know them. They were all well known, actually much better known than I was. I was the new kid on the block, and they were all preaching at the conference.

They were saying all kinds of different things, and every time they did worship, they had people come out and do Jewish dances. They had Jewish music, and all their songs were begging God to come, to show up, to touch us, and to bless us.

Right behind me was a big sign that said, "Except your Spirit go with me, I will not go." There was a huge, beautiful Ark of the Covenant replica made up. It was about as big as a pulpit. Every preacher there got behind it and preached.

I was waiting for them to tell me when I was going to preach. We had some of our people there, and I told them, "I am not preaching behind that Ark." I said, "I will not do it." I said, "They will move that Ark out of there, because a New Covenant Ark is not going to stand behind an Old Covenant Ark to preach."

I didn't announce it. I didn't tell the Moderator of the meeting; I didn't say anything to him about it. I just told our people. The amazing thing was, by the Spirit of God, just before I got up to preach, the leader of the group, the Moderator there, said, "Do you know what? I believe we should move that Ark."

They moved that Ark off the platform and moved it toward a door. When they got it over there, they set it down, and we started the meetings. I said, "You almost took it far enough, but it's still in the same room." I said, "You need to get it out of here."

I explained to them how we carry the Spirit of God and how we are His representation. I have said before that I get invited to a lot of places one time. That was one of them. I've never been invited back.

When I got up, I said, "We're out here in the middle of nowhere. You don't get here by accident. You have to have a purpose to come here." I said, "Now, imagine if someone who was seeking God, not born again, didn't have the Spirit of God, but they wanted God, and they desired God, came in.

I said, "If they were looking for God, and they came in through the front door while we were worshipping, what would they think? Would they think, 'Wow, these people know God,' or would they think, 'These people are looking for God just like I am, but they haven't found Him yet.' Based on the worship and the music, obviously, you haven't found Him, yet."

I said, "I'm here to tell you, He's in me. He walks in me; He lives in me." I went through the whole thing. For two sessions, several hours, I just killed their sacred cows, and I told them truth about our union with Christ, and how He walks in us, talks in us, lives through us, and we are complete in Him.

I want to share a few things with you, and then, I want you to take your Bible and go with me to a few places. I promise not to preach and preach. When I just stand up and share, this is what comes out. This is normal. This is life. It isn't a sermon to me.

When I started, I had a daughter that was very sick. She had a tumour, and when she was two years and three months, she passed away. I tried to reach everybody that was teaching me faith. I tried to get them on the telephone, but I couldn't get anyone to answer. I couldn't reach them or talk to them, and I kept trying to find someone.

I had heard all of these stories, but I was trying to find someone who could actually do what I'd heard them talk about. I was looking for somebody that could raise my daughter from the dead, and I couldn't find anybody. The next day, we buried her. When I stood at that grave, I told God, "God, there was no man for me when I needed one, but if You will teach me, I will be that man for somebody else."

The reason I'm telling you this is because I want you to know that we've seen nine or so come back from the dead. We have seen thousands of healings. We have seen everything. We've seen every part of the human body healed. We've seen every kind of disease defeated. It has been amazing!

What I have found out is that no disease matters. What they have never matters. Never focus on what they have, just focus on what you have, because what you have is greater than what they have. I never focus on the disease.

I don't care what you tell me, because you cannot come up with anything that either has a name, or doesn't have a name, that is going to be bigger than what I've got. Who I have in me is the God of the universe. He is more powerful than anything else. It is by His Spirit that we do what we do. You can't intimidate me through sickness, or disease or anything else, because I know Who is in me.

I walk into hospital rooms, and go into contagious wards. I've done that all over the world now, and I've laid my hands on people with all kinds of contagious diseases. I have put my face in front of people that were breathing out airborne or contagious diseases. I've had people spit on me, and sweat on me, and I've never caught anything from any of them, because as soon as it touches me, it must die.

Death must be swallowed up in life! Amen? Our job is just to find out what life we have. We need to let that life emanate from us, consume all of the death and destruction, and all of the evil in this world, and just kill it.

I don't know if you have heard or not, but I'm the general overseer of John G. Lake Ministries. When John Lake was here (in South Africa) from 1908 to 1913, there was a plague going on that the people were dying from.

They were dying by the thousands, and he went into an affected area. Some of the doctors asked him, "How can you be in here? You shouldn't be here. This could kill you." Some of their doctors were dying, but many of Dr. Lake's workers never caught it.

They asked, "How are you doing this?" He said, "Well, watch. Let me show you." He said, "Go get the foam from the dead person's mouth." They got the foam and looked at it under a microscope. They took it, and put it in Dr. Lake's hand. He held it for just a couple of seconds. He didn't pray or do anything. He just held it, and then gave it back to them. They looked at it again, under a microscope, and every disease germ had died.

They said, "This is impossible. How did you do this?" He said, "Oh, it's very simple. The law of the Spirit of life in Christ Jesus has made me free from the law of sin and death." He understood that when sickness, death, disease, killing, stealing, and destroying of human life got near him, it had to die.

We don't always understand that the creative power of God is also destructive. It will destroy the works of the devil. Amen? You have to get a grasp of the fact that, not only do you have life that can re-create limbs and re-create organs, but you also have a life that destroys sickness and disease.

Jesus said, in Luke 10:1-7, that He sent out his disciples, and He told them, "Whatever city you go into, heal the sick in the city." That means you don't go in there and find believers, and just pray for believers. He said, "Find the sick. Go looking for the sick."

We have this thing that is wrong in the church. We think that the sick should find us. The sick shouldn't find us any easier than demon possessed people should find us. If a person is demon possessed, do you think the demon wants the person free? Of course he doesn't.

What makes you think that the demon is going to let the person get to you? They'll keep him busy. They'll make him run out, and hide, and get away from you. Sometimes you have to sneak up on the devil, because if he knows you're coming, he'll run.

We were listening to a pastor the other day that said he would say to his sons, "Get up, we're going to go do a crusade." They would say, "Where are we going?" He'd say, "We're going north." They'd all get in the van, and they would take off, and he would go east. They would say, "Dad, this isn't north, this is east." He would say, "Yeah, I know. I just told you that so the devil would hear it, and he would go north to try to defend it." Now, that's strategy.

What you have to realize is that sickness and disease is an enemy. We shouldn't wait for it to find us. We ought to go find it. If there are sick in your city, it's your fault. It's not the devil's fault. He's doing whatever he can do. That's his job, if you want to call it that.

When you go into a city, and there's sickness there, it is because believers are not searching out and destroying all of the works of the enemy. They're not going into the city and healing the sick that are there, and then telling them, "The kingdom of heaven is at hand." That's what He said to do.

We have all of these religious things built up so that we think it has to be like this and like that, and people have to believe, and then they have to do it a certain way. Let me tell you, "You should have faith for other people. You shouldn't worry about their faith."

They're unbelievers. What makes you think they have faith? You shouldn't worry. Unbelievers are not required to have faith. That's why they're unbelievers. If they had faith, they'd be believers. They're unbelievers. You have faith for them.

We are the ones that are told that we have power and authority over all sickness, disease, and over all devils. It doesn't say you have power and authority over sickness and devils as long as the person believes. That's not real authority. If I have authority, I have authority.

If I have authority over sickness and disease, that means I have authority over all sickness and all disease, no matter where they are, even if they're living in your body. If they're living in your body, I can tell them to go, and they will go. Why? It is because I have authority over them.

People say, "Well, what about that person's will?" Show me in the Bible where it says anything about the person's will. Most sick people want to get well, so I'm not going against their will. The only will I'm going against is the devil's will. He wants to stay there, but I have authority over his will. I have authority over sickness and disease, as well as you do, if you're a believer. We have that authority.

Just because that sickness or disease is in a person, it does not negate your authority. If that were true, you wouldn't truly have authority over anybody but yourself, and it doesn't say you have authority over yourself. It says you have authority over sickness, disease, and demons. You've just got to learn to read the Word, and believe exactly what it says. If it says, "You have authority over sickness and disease," you do. Act like it.

I'm going to look at a few more verses, and then I'm going to read some things to you. In the DHT manual, I have some letters and a few other things that Dr. Lake wrote. I won't read them all, but I'll read a couple of them to you.

In Luke 4:18, it says,

> 18 The Spirit of the Lord is upon me because He has anointed me.

Why is the Spirit upon you? It is because you're anointed. The Spirit upon you is not what anoints you. It doesn't say, "I'm anointed because the Spirit is upon me." It says, "The Spirit is upon me, because I am anointed." That means you were anointed before the Spirit came upon you. That changes everything. Believe me, it changes the way you pray for people.

Go with me to Galatians 3:29. It says,

> 29 And if you be Christ's then are you Abraham's seed, and heirs according to the promise.

If you are Christ's, if you belong to Him, you are Abraham's seed. The seed that he was talking to are those that are the seed by faith in Christ Jesus, so obviously, He wasn't talking of nationality. The seed of Abraham are those who are in Christ Jesus by faith of Christ Jesus. It says, "Then are you Abraham's seed, and heirs according to the promise."

In Galatians 4:1 it says,

> 1 Now I say, That the heir, as long as he is a child, differeth nothing from a servant, though he be lord of all;

Who's the heir? You are. The child who is spiritually immature and carnal minded is no different than a servant. In other words, under this New Testament that we have, the child here would differ nothing from an Old Testament saint. That shows you, and gives you an idea that the child is like them. In other words, think about the Old Testament saints.

All of the prophets and the people in the Old Testament were great men and women of God. You must realize that the heir, as long as he is a child, is like them, before he is grown up. Now, he's even better than that.

He is saying that the heir, as long as he is immature, as long as he is spiritually immature and a babe in Christ and not grown up, he is going to act, think, talk, and do everything just like those Old Testament saints did. It means that the heirs are going to talk about the moving of the Spirit. It means they are going to talk about the Spirit coming upon them. They are going to talk about all of these different things and how the anointing would come upon them at times, like it did Samson. We have to realize, that is not us.

We are not people upon whom the Spirit comes at times, because there is never a time, if you're born of God and born of Christ, that you do not have His Spirit. The best way to get the Spirit upon you is to let Him out. When you let Him out, there is that aspect of being in the presence of God, which is a tangible presence that you can sense, feel, and experience. That is all fine and good; especially good for church.

My calling, predominantly, is to equip you, not for church, but for the world, because Jesus didn't say, "Go ye into all the church." He said, "Go ye into all the world." We must take Christ to the world.

By taking Christ to the world, that means I am assuming certain things. That means that I am assuming that you want to walk in power; that you want to walk in Christ; that you want to walk in the Spirit, to live in the Spirit, and to be in the Spirit.

I am assuming that you're not like many who just want to use God, or use Jesus, for fire insurance to keep you out of hell, or for an escape clause to get you out of here. If you're one of those, I really don't have a lot for you. I really will not waste my time on people who are just trying to use God to guarantee them blissfulness.

The people that I'm speaking to and those that are hearing the voice of the Spirit in what I say, are those who say, "I am so thankful to God that He has saved me, delivered me, and changed me, that I want to do something for Him. I want to be what He has called me to be. I know that He has changed me, like in the song, 'He Has Changed My Heart,' so because of that, I want to live in the fullness of everything that is promised."

If that's you, you are the one I'm talking to. My purpose in being here is to equip you, to make you more effective for the street, not just to give you another teaching. You didn't have to come all this way just to get another teaching. Amen? The idea is that we do something that will work; something that will change the world.

My job is to help you get from being a child to growing up into the things of God. There are various aspects that we teach on the difference between milk and meat. I'm going to give you the short version. Meat is the Word that you do. In the Bible is milk. There is no meat; there is milk. It even tells you, "Desire the sincere milk of the Word." It never really talks about meat being in this written Word, but when you take the milk and you start doing the milk, then the milk will become meat.

The meat is the doing. In John 4:32, Jesus said, "I have meat that you know not of." He said, "My meat is to do the will of Him who sent me," so meat, spiritual meat, is doing the will of God. Get the thought out of your mind, "This is milk, and some day, maybe, God will give me the meat." Today is the day.

I am always making notes about different things, and some of these things just stick with me. This is especially true when it comes to talking about manifesting sons of God. We have to realize that there's a lot of talk in the church about manifestations, yet we are the manifestation that the Bible talks about.

We are to manifest as sons of God. We are to show forth ourselves as sons of God. It is not a matter of waiting for a time for it to happen. Is the world groaning for it? Yes. The whole earth and the whole creation are groaning for manifestation. They are waiting, but it doesn't say they are waiting for a certain time. It says that they are waiting for us to manifest, so don't wait.

You decide when to manifest. You decide how quickly you grow. You decide how quickly you want to just believe the Word, and do it. When you do it, He will abide in you and manifest Himself through you, and you will be manifesting as a son.

There are some things that we are going to talk about concerning Dr. Lake. One of the things I loved about Dr. Lake was the fact that he knew that we're seated in heaven; no doubt about it. There is the truth of being seated in heaven, and yet we're on the earth. There is a truth there.

At the same time, we have to realize that if we are to have the fullness of God in us, if we are going to manifest the fullness of God like Jesus did, then there is a connection between heaven and us. However, it is not a connection where we're waiting on heaven to send the power through.

Is God still pouring out His Spirit like we hear today? Yes, He's still pouring out His Spirit, and those that are hungry and thirsty need to grasp it, and hold on to it. There comes a point when you just come to the realization, "I've got it. This is who I am," then you start speaking that way, singing that way, and talking that way.

You have to ask, "Do I need more?" The Epistles are full of things that we need to add to our faith and add to our knowledge. We need to add all of these things that we are continually growing in, because we are going to "grow up into Him in all things, which are the head, even Christ." (Ephesians 4:15) We are going to grow up into Him, but at the same time, we have to realize that we are growing in Him, also.

The growing in Him is the constantly being filled. There is a process where you should continually be filled. In Jude chapter 1, verse 20, it tells us to build ourselves up in our most holy faith, praying in the Holy Ghost. There is a building up in that. There is work that still needs to be done in us so that we grow up in Him, but we also need to realize that there is a point when we must "grow up into Him." That is where our maturity is.

In Galatians 4:1, it says, "The heir, as long as he is a child..." You are the heir. As long as you're under the Law, still carnally minded and fleshly minded, then you are a child, and you "differ nothing from a servant, though he (this heir, this child) is lord of all."

Who's lord of all? "The heir is the lord of all." Most people would say, "Well, that's Jesus." Yes, but you're joint heirs with Him, so whatever He has, you have. You're not co-heirs. To be co-heirs means half and half. Joint heirs means that everything He has, you have.

The Bible says that He is King of kings, and we know we're the kings He's King over, because God has made us kings and priests unto our God. We also know that He is Lord of lords, but who are the lords is He Lord over? We are. If we are the lords that He's Lord over, and He's Lord over all, and we have everything He has, then we are lord over all.

It says, "As long as that heir is a child, he differs nothing from a servant, though he be lord of all." During that time, he is under tutors and governors until the time appointed of the Father. If you look in Galatians 3:25, it says,

> 25 But after that faith is come, we are no longer under a schoolmaster.

That means you are no longer under a tutor. This is the time to grow up. This is the time to walk in the fullness of what God has provided through Jesus Christ.

It says, in Galatians 4:3,

> 3 Even so we, when we were children, were in bondage under the elements of the world:

If you're not a child, you're not under bondage to the elements of the world. What are the elements of the world? Well, weather is. You tell it what to do. You say, "Can we do that?" Yes. The same works that Jesus did, you can do, and He calmed the sea. You can tell crops to grow or to die, as the case may be. He spoke to a fig tree. You can speak to crops.

I will give you the example of a man I know that lives in a place in Mexico where a plague of locusts came in and tore up everybody's crops, except for his crop in the middle.

The locusts jumped over that crop and left it alone, and it was because this man understood the grace of God. He understood that he was protected and wasn't under the beggarly elements of this world.

The Bible says, "A thousand will fall at your left hand and ten thousand at your right, but it won't come near you." (Psalm 91:7). People say, "These are Old Testament promises." How much more so should it be for you?

What you have to do is switch from the, "I'm going to make it," to the, "Thank you Jesus for putting me there." That's not to say that you've attained, but you are in a place of completion. Now, you just have to live up to it.

The way that you start realizing your place of completion is through the renewal of the mind. He recreated your spirit. It was made perfect and complete, but you have to renew the mind. That's your job.

Any hindrance is not on the part of God; it's not even on the part of the devil. It is your laziness that keeps you from renewing your mind, so you've got no one to blame except yourself. It's as simple as that.

He goes on to say in Galatians 4:4-6,

> 4 But when the fulness of the time was come, God sent forth his Son, made of a woman, made under the law,
>
> 5 To redeem them that were under the law, that we might receive the adoption of sons.
>
> 6 And because ye are sons, God hath sent forth the Spirit of his Son into your hearts, crying, Abba, Father.

We just read Luke 4:18, "The Spirit of the Lord is upon me because he has anointed me." It says in John 1:12,

> 12 To as many as received Him, gave He authority to become the sons of God.

In 1 John 3:2, it says,

> 2 Beloved, now are we the sons and God, and it doth not yet appear what we shall be, but we know that when He shall appear, we shall be like Him.

When are you going to be a son of God? The time is right now. He even said, "Behold what manner of love that the Father has bestowed upon us that we should be called the sons of God." We're sons now! You've already made the big step. Now, your job is to make one small step, and that is just to manifest.

It doesn't say that everybody has to become sons. It says that the earth is waiting for the manifestation of the sons. In other words, it knows the sons are here. It's just waiting for us to manifest. It's just waiting for us to choose to show up, and to speak whenever something bad is going on. In the crowd, a son should step forward, and say, "Wait just a minute. This doesn't have to be this way."

What is happening when he steps in and says that? That is a son that is manifesting. We have seen it in bits and pieces. We have seen it in men like John Lake and Smith Wigglesworth. They operated in it at points, but they didn't walk it. Our job is to walk it. We are going to walk in the fullness of it.

"Because He has anointed me, the Spirit of the Lord is upon me." He has anointed me, because I am a son. "God has sent forth the Spirit of His son." You were anointed when you got born again. That is the anointing.

What I want you to see is this: the minute you got born again, you were appointed and anointed. Being appointed and anointed are the same thing. To be appointed is to be anointed, and to be anointed is to be appointed. You are appointed a son of God. You were anointed a son of God.

All of the kings of Israel were anointed as kings. They didn't change in the sense that all of a sudden they had supernatural powers. That means that each was set apart, at a point in time, to be king.

As a matter of fact, if you go through and read all of the Scriptures about anoint this and anoint that, or set this apart, it always has to do with setting apart someone to be put into a position. It never talks, especially in the Old Testament, about power. It never talks about getting power, and it never talks about operating in power.

The closest it comes to saying that is when someone was anointed, and then it says they had the spirit of wisdom, because then they were anointed to do something, and when they were anointed to do it, they were put in that position, and God would give them the Spirit of wisdom to accomplish that. Go back, and study it. We're just throwing some lifelines out there for you to get hold of. Go back and study, and prove it out, and teach it from there.

We know that the minute you got born again, you were anointed and appointed. We know that before a person could be born again, Jesus had to die and pour out His blood. When He gave up the blood that bought us our position in God, at that moment and from that point on, you could be born again. Before that, Jesus talked about them becoming sons of God, and then He poured out His blood, which gave them the ability to become sons of God; the authority to become sons of God.

We read in Acts 1:8,

> 8 But you shall receive power, after the Holy Ghost is come upon you.

We have got two situations. Number one: we have to be born again. Number two: we have to have the Spirit come upon us. He said, "You shall receive power," and that word for *power* is the word *ability*. *Miraculous ability* is actually what it means. It says, "You will receive *miraculous ability* after the Holy Ghost is come upon you."

We've got two instances here. We've got you getting born again, appointed, anointed as a son, and being put into a position as a son. Galatians 4:6 says, "And because you are sons, God hath sent forth the Spirit of His Son into your hearts crying, 'Abba, Father.'"

First you're born again, and then the Spirit comes upon you. Because you are anointed, the Spirit is upon you. That's what Jesus meant when He said, "The Spirit is upon me, because I'm anointed." I know I'm drilling this in, but this is a total opposite turn around from what has been taught in the church, as a whole, for about 100 years or so.

John Alexander Dowie had a tremendous healing ministry without ever receiving the Baptism of the Spirit. Why? It is because he saw Scriptures that said that healing is right.

John Lake had a very tremendous healing ministry before he ever received the Baptism of the Spirit. You say, "Then why do we need the Baptism of the Spirit?" First of all, when you get born again, you become a son and have authority. You have everything you need, right then, to do anything you need to do, especially with your own life. However, when you get that Spirit that comes upon you, that Spirit is sent into your heart crying, "Abba, Father."

That Baptism in the Spirit is what Acts 1:8 and Acts 2:4 speak of. When that happens, you can act like a son anytime, anywhere, under any circumstances, without having to be told what to do; without having to be led to do it. You will not find one place in the New Testament where it ever said that anybody was led to heal the sick, led to raise the dead, or led to preach. It never says that.

There are two places where it talks about being led by the Spirit. One is in Matthew, and another is in Luke, where it says, "Jesus was led of the Spirit out into the wilderness to be tested or tempted of the devil."

That's not a leading that most people want to try to claim. As a matter of fact, most of you don't need it. You're drawn away of your own lust. You really don't need to be led by the Spirit to go and find your sin. You can find it on your own, so we don't generally claim that one.

There is another Scripture in Romans 8:14 where it says,

> 14 For as many as are led by the Spirit of God, they are the sons of God.

It's not saying, as the church has taught in the past, "At times, the Spirit moves me to go pray for the sick, and do works." That's not what it's talking about. You have to read it in context.

All of Romans 8 has nothing to do with praying for the sick or doing any work. It is talking about you mortifying the deeds of the flesh; every one of them. It is not talking about you being led to go to the grocery store to pray for somebody or something like that.

Jesus talked about the Spirit of truth in John 16:13, when He said,

> 13 Howbeit when he, the Spirit of truth, is come, he will guide you into all truth: for he shall not speak of himself; but whatsoever he shall hear, that shall he speak: and he will shew you things to come.

"When the Spirit of truth is come, He will guide you into all truth." He didn't say He was going to lead you into healing the sick. He didn't say He was going to lead you to do anything. He said He would lead you into truth. When you learn truth, then moral obligation should lead you to walk in that truth. The minute you know truth, you must walk in it. "Well, I'm waiting for God to quicken it to me." The Bible doesn't say that. It doesn't say that He is going to quicken His Word to you, and you only have to obey what Word He quickens.

The Bible says that you're responsible for every bit of this. As a matter of fact, the minute you heard about it, you became responsible for it. You were responsible even before you heard about it, because it was your job to find out what it said, not wait for somebody else to tell you. You need to realize that the Spirit of God has come for a specific purpose. It has come to lead and guide you into truth.

If you are going to be a son of God, then you shouldn't need any outside source moving you to do anything. Your spirit and God's Spirit are the same. They mix. "He that is joined to the Lord is one Spirit with the Lord." It is not a matter of, "Well, the Spirit has to tell me, and I have to…" No. When He thinks it, I think it. There's no delay. We are one.

When you think of Jesus, you don't think of Jesus as being separate. You think of Jesus as having such total union with the Holy Spirit and with God the Father that there's no differentiation; yet Jesus prayed to the Father, and He talked about the Holy Spirit. He said, "When the Holy Spirit comes, He's not going to talk about Himself; He's going to talk about me." He said, "He will tell you all things that I've said; He will bring to your remembrance what I've said."

When you think of that Scripture, you think, "Was that me, or was that God?" Well, first of all, you shouldn't even think that way. You ought to know you are one with Him. That's the Holy Spirit bringing to remembrance what He said, so whenever you see a sick person, and you remember Mark 16 that says, "Believers will lay hands on the sick, and they will recover," that is not you. That is the Spirit of God, in you, reminding you.

If He reminds you, then obviously, you're supposed to do it. It's not a leading. It's a remembrance. You don't need to be led to heal the sick. You should remember what the Lord said, and do it. His nature and His character should drive you to do what is supposed to be done.

One time Jesus talked to his disciples, and He said, "I'm not going to call you servants. I'm going to call you friends." Why? It is because a servant doesn't know what his master does, but a son knows his father's will. Now, at that time, He couldn't call them sons, because they weren't born again. Calling them friends was as close as He could get.

We sing the song, "I Am a Friend of God." I'm not a friend of God. I'm a son. That's closer than a friend. It says, "There is One that sticketh closer, even than a brother." It's closer than being a friend. We are sons. You might tell a friend, "Sorry, I can't help you," but you won't tell that to a son. The son knows that whatever you have, he has.

Our problem is that we don't want to take our place as sons. We want to stay in that position of servant. We want them to say, "Well, now we're going to welcome this servant of God."

I've had that introduction so many times, and it's always embarrassing, because then I have to turn right around and tell the people, "I'm sorry. I'm not a servant of God. I'm a son who serves." There's a difference between being a servant and being a son that serves. Do I serve God? Yes. Am I a servant of God? No. Why? Even in Galatians 4:7 it told us, saying,

> 7 Wherefore thou art no more a servant, but a son; and if a son, then an heir of God through Christ.

"Wherefore you are no more servants, but sons," so when someone says that they are a servant, it just shows that they don't read the Bible. We are sons.

Every time you hear the Gospel, it should always make you make a choice. Unless you are constantly walking as a fully manifested son of God, with no room to grow, you have two options. You can remain the same or change. That's it. For sons, there's really only one option and that is to change. You do not have the option, the luxury to not change, when you hear truth.

If that's you, to not change when you hear truth, then you would be similar to those who would draw back, those who would have heard the Gospel and would have become like those in Hebrews 5, who have need of milk and not meat. That is because, "where by reason of time," you should be teaching others, and now you need somebody to teach you the very basics all over again. The reason those people got in that position is because they refused to move forward, and they kept going back under the Law.

What you have to realize is that you may be well versed in not going back under the Law, but you also must be well versed in not going back into religion. This means that hearing the Word cannot satisfy you. You can't just say, "Wow, that was a good message," or "That really made me think." No.

It says, "You are not to be hearers only, but doers of the Word." You must be doers of the Word. That means you must begin doing what you hear immediately, or else you have a danger of falling back into the "just preaching" mode.

I can tell you, "I do not just preach." I hope you understand that I don't come here just to preach; I didn't need to come here just to preach. I can be anywhere in the world preaching; anytime. I don't just do sermons. I do training.

My purpose is to equip the body of Christ to "grow up into Him in all things." Now, healing happens to be the thing that we are known for, because we have great success in that area. God has shown us a few things that work extremely well.

As you probably already know, there are many groups out there that will claim some type of association with John Lake. There are people that will claim that they're doing things like John Lake did, but I will tell you this: the family passed the ministry to me.

I do not reverence John Lake. He was a man of God, and he did a great work, but he was a man. He didn't die on a cross for me, and so I don't elevate him in that way. Do I respect him and give him honor? Yes, but this is not about John Lake. This is about Jesus Christ. It is about you understanding that it is Christ in you, the "hope of glory." It is not John Lake in you.

The reason I said that is because there are groups out there that are trying to claim association with him, but he gave a prophecy in 1934 that related information about the person that would take on his ministry and carry it according to his words; to greater depths.

Over a period of time, after my daughter died, I was looking for answers. I started searching, and I heard about men like Wigglesworth, and John Lake, and others. Of all the people, John Lake interested me the most. He not only did it, but he taught people how to do it, and they had the same results, and in some cases, greater results than he had.

I knew that a man that could not only do it, but could teach it, and the people that he taught could do it, I knew that man knew more about what he was talking about than just a person that preaches.

I started searching him out. I found out that he died in 1935, and I was not happy. It seemed like every time I found a hero, he was already dead.

I kept on searching, and I found his family. I found his daughter Gertrude and her husband, Wilford Reidt. I started calling them in 1981 and started up a relationship with them. They lived in Kennewick, Washington, and I had a relationship with them for about seven years.

Gertrude passed away in November 1986, and I knew Wilfred wouldn't last that much longer. He was missing her so much; I could hear it in his voice.

He and I started talking about various other aspects of the ministry, not just about John Lake. I was asking questions, and then, he started asking me about my testimony. After I gave him my testimony and told him all the details of my life, he finally said, "I want to give the ministry to you."

Many of you probably don't know that a car ran over me when I was seventeen months old. My father backed over me in the driveway. It ripped off my right ear, ripped my scalp from one side to the other, and my scalp was pulled down like a mask to my eyes.

It took 172 stitches and 6 hours of surgery to do what they could to put it all back together. The doctor said I wouldn't live, so my mom went to praying. She said, "God, I dedicate him to you; he's yours. Let him live."

The doctor came out in a little while, and said, "It looks like he might live, but if he does he'll be a vegetable all the days of his life. You'll have to feed him, and clothe him, and take care of him." The doctor went back to work, and my mom went back to praying. She said, "God, that's not good enough. If you're going to let him live, let him be normal."

As I always tell everybody, there's a lot of discussion over whether I'm normal or not, but I'm not concerned about it, because it's working for me. Amen?

A little while later, the doctor came out, and said, "We haven't found any signs of brain damage, but even if he doesn't have brain damage, even if he lives, he will never have any hearing in his right ear, and he will never have any hair." He went back to work.

My mom went back to praying. She said, "God, that's not good enough." I was an only child. My mother was not supposed to be able to have children.

My mom kept me at home, so I didn't start school right away. Actually, I started learning at the right time, because instead of sending me to kindergarten, she kept me at home and started teaching me to read using the King James Bible. By the time I started school, we had already read through the Bible seven or eight times.

My dad worked at night, and my mom would, in the beginning, read the Bible until I fell asleep. As we got older, once I started reading, she would have me read the Bible to her until she fell asleep. I am always blessed, because I tell everybody, "I'm still reading people to sleep with the Bible. It still works today."

The fact is, that because of that (I didn't know it at the time) God was putting His Word in me. I have a recall of Scripture that is very beneficial to what I am doing today, and the Holy Spirit brings to remembrance Scripture and different things at different times. I will have a question, and He'll give me a Scripture.

After I gave Wilfred my testimony, I said, "I don't know when I got hit. I will have to call my mom to find out the dates." He said, "Well, call and find out." I called her, and she said it was September 16, 1960. I called him back, and he said, "Yes, that's what I thought."

I said, "What do you mean, 'That's what you thought?' Why would you think that?" He said, "Well, there's this prophecy that John Lake gave on May 24, 1934, and I believe that it applies to you." He said, "Let me read it to you," and he started reading it to me.

It said that the person that would take up John Lake's ministry would be born the year the country quit growing. The last state was added to the United States in 1959. That's the year I was born, April 1, 1959.

Later on, it said that Satan would try to kill this person 25 years to the day from Dr. Lake's death. I was run over on September 16, 1960. If you go back 25 years, to that date of September 16, 1935, that is the day John Lake passed away.

Because of my background, Wilfred said, "I believe, based on the answers to the questions that the ministry should go to you." I didn't ask him about the anointing. I didn't ask him about all the things that people try to ask about like, "How do I get his anointing." I didn't ask any of that.

I asked, "How did he pray? What did he say? What did he believe? What did he preach?" I asked those questions, because I knew that the answers to those were the secret.

It wasn't just an anointing that John Lake had. It wasn't something God just dumped on him. He had sixteen brothers and sisters, and by the time he was 21, eight of them had died due to sickness. He was fed up. He had to have an answer, and he started seeking God. He said, "I want to learn healing."

Dr. Lake heard about this man named, John Alexander Dowie, and he said, "This man is having great success." He said to his wife, "I'm going to study divine healing under Dowie so that I can learn it, and teach it." He learned divine healing.

Later, he opened his famous healing rooms in Spokane (which have not been in existence for the last 65 years). The Healing Rooms, in the original healing room building, the Rookery building, was destroyed by fire in the late '30s. That was after John Lake passed away.

A new building was built, and John Lake never set foot in that building. There have been a lot of different rumors and stories passed around that are not true. Besides, God is not interested in shrines. You don't need to get an anointing by rubbing the wood.

The anointing you need is the one you have, which is the anointing of Jesus. It is His Spirit. John Lake didn't even have a John Lake anointing, because there are not different kinds of anointing. There is one anointing, and that is the Spirit of Jesus. It is manifested in different ways, but it's all Jesus. You have what you need.

The only other thing you might need is to know how to release it, which is what we do. We teach you how to release it and use what you have. If you understand that, you'll realize that it's not about chasing something. It is about you getting out of the way so that what you have can work. Mark 16:15-18 says,

> 15 And he said unto them, Go ye into all the world, and preach the gospel to every creature.
>
> 16 He that believeth and is baptized shall be saved; but he that believeth not shall be damned.

17 And these signs shall follow them that believe; In my name shall they cast out devils; they shall speak with new tongues;

18 They shall take up serpents; and if they drink any deadly thing, it shall not hurt them; they shall lay hands on the sick, and they shall recover.

"These signs shall follow those that believe." It goes on to say, "In my name shall they cast out devils; they shall speak with new tongues; they shall take up serpents; and if they drink any deadly thing it shall not hurt them; they shall lay hands on the sick, and they shall recover." These are some of the signs that are to follow believers.

I told you at the beginning that I went to this place to preach, and it had that big sign behind me that said, "Except your Spirit go with me, I will not go." The sad part is that people don't understand progressive revelation, because when they said that, that was what they believed.

That is not the truth that was still in force even as late as King David. King David knew better than that. He said, "If I go down to the very depths, where can I go that your Spirit is not there? If I go to the highest heavens, where can I go that your Spirit is not there?" (Psalm 139:7-8). Even King David knew that there is nowhere you can go that the Spirit of God is not there.

Even today, we have so called Christian television preaching about where the presence is. It tells you, "You have got to get your offering in by a certain time or else your offering won't be accepted, because the Spirit of God is going to be over this offering." Where can you go that the Spirit of God is not there?

Do you realize that the Spirit of God is in the HIV ward at the hospital? You say, "Then, why aren't the people healed?" It is because the Spirit doesn't have a "hand" to lay on them. He's there; He's just waiting for a Christian to show up that He can put on like a glove, in that sense, and put His hands on. That's the reason.

How to enter the will of God is going to be in keeping with the theme of this message. I will be dealing with walking in the Spirit and understanding some of the things of the Spirit realm. If you'll catch some of the wording here, I guarantee you, it will change your life. It will change your ministry, and even greater than that, it will change the lives of all of those around you.

Dr. Lake says that there are two phases to entering into the will of God. The first phase is the surrender of your will to do the will of God. That's the first step. Now, I am assuming that if you're ministers and believers that you have done that. You have surrendered your will to do the will of God.

Most people's conception of doing the will of God is to become a non-entity. That means that most people's idea of getting into the will of God means, "Well, I'm just going to void my mind and have no desires; nothing. I'm going to just fast, and I'm just going to put my body under. I'm just going to beat it down. I want no desire. I'm going to void my mind, and I'm just going to let the Spirit move me."

That is not Biblical; it is not Christian. It is New Age or Eastern religion. Nowhere are you told to void your mind. First of all, there is no such thing as a void. If you try to void your mind, I promise you, you will get devils. There is no void. The Bible doesn't say to void your mind. It says, "Renew your mind." That doesn't mean take everything out; it means replace everything.

You have to replace the old mind with the mind of Christ. The mind of Christ is not void. The mind of Christ has all the riches of wisdom, and revelation, and understanding. It has all the understanding of the power of God and how it works. It's all there. Don't void your mind; renew your mind. Amen? Don't become a non-entity, and float around. Do something.

That's one of the things that I see so often in some of the conferences I've gone to, especially in the States. The epitome of the conference is when everybody falls out, which isn't even talked about in the Bible that much. As a matter of fact, the only people you find falling out around Jesus were non-believers. The Romans, the temple guard, and people like that fell down.

People that came to arrest Him fell down. Why did they fall down, and all of His disciples didn't? His disciples were all there. Why doesn't it say everybody fell down? It was because the ones who had come to arrest Jesus had not been around the Spirit of God.

Believe me; I'm not against people falling out, as long as it is of God. If you want to fall out, fine. I have no problem with that. The question that people ask is, "If I fall, why don't you fall?"

Co-Workers With God

If I'm the one delivering and it hits me first, shouldn't I fall out before you get it? As a minister of God, a representative of Jesus Christ, you must learn that you are a carrier. I don't like to say it this way, but maybe you'll get the idea. You are insulated; you are ground. It flows through you to hit them, but doesn't hit you. Now, you may be affected, but it doesn't hit you like it does them. Why? It is because you get used to it, and you should.

One thing that bothers me the most is when I go to meetings where everybody falls out. It is amazing how the Holy Spirit shows up in such force. However, the Holy Spirit doesn't show up just for you to fall down. He comes in for a purpose. He comes in to touch, and heal, and deliver, and set free, and to give you wisdom and understanding and gifts and all of those things. He comes in with a purpose, and yet we think that when He shows up, we should all fall down.

I picture the Holy Spirit walking into a room, and everybody falling out, and then Him saying, "I was just fixing to start working in some of you. How am I going to get any work done with all of my workers laid out on the floor?" We think it is the epitome of spirituality to fall out. It doesn't impress me when people fall out. It impresses me when you get the job done that you were called to do. Amen?

It's amazing how many people fall out in church, and they never fall out in the grocery store. Do you know why? There are two reasons: no carpet (floors are usually concrete) and no catchers.

It is not God's idea for you to have to be pushed around like a machine or moved like a mechanism. Suppose you are walking through the grocery store, with your shopping cart, and all of a sudden you walk past a sick person. When you're walking past them, you think, "If God wants me to pray for them, He'll take my hand, and place it on them." No, that would be like God being the puppet master and you being the puppet, and you just putting your hand over there, and saying, "Well, okay. I guess He wants me to pray for you." That's not God's idea. That would be like if you were a child and were told what and how to do it.

You're supposed to be manifesting as sons of God. Jesus wouldn't have acted like that. He always walked with purpose. He always ministered with purpose. He didn't just walk past people, and say, "Oh, it must be you." No, Jesus didn't minister that way.

Dr. Lake said that the other phase, phase two, is recognizing your own self as God's son and man's servant. I tell everybody, "There are three things you need to know: first, you are God's son, second, you are the devil's master, and third, you are man's servant."

You're not God's servant; you're man's servant. You're God's son, the devil's master, and man's servant. You can't be man's servant and get sickness off of them until you're the devil's master, and you can't be the devil's master until you are God's son.

As God's son, the devil's master, and man's servant, you can heal the world. Why? It is because no devil can stand before you all the days of your life, because, "Greater is He that's in you, than he that is in the world."

John Lake wrote the following: "I think the most wonderful exhibition of this truth that God can give us, is in the fact that He gives us the Holy Ghost to use for God." Isn't that the opposite of what we've heard in the church most of the time? "Well, we are to give ourselves to God." There is truth to that, but the Word says, "They received the Holy Ghost." That means, you understand, that He didn't get them; they got Him.

We always think, "Well, I am His, so He can do whatever He wants." That's not what the Bible says. The Bible says that you are His, because you believe in Jesus Christ. You're born again; born of His Spirit. His Spirit is in you. The Spirit of power is there to manifest, and it's for you to operate; for you to use for God.

This is what John Lake understood. This is what is so radically different about his message. Dr. Lake said, "The Lord says they shall lay hands on the sick, and they shall recover, but if you do not lay your hands upon anyone, they will not be healed."

Who is the world waiting on? Is the world waiting on God? No. Do you think God's just sitting there, saying, "Well, what time is it? No, not time to move yet." Do you think that's what He's doing? No.

What is the world waiting for? Is it waiting for the manifestation of the sons of God? "The whole earth groans; all of creation groans; waiting." Why? It is under bondage of sickness, disease, decay, and all of the things that are going on. It's waiting for the manifestation of the sons of God.

God is waiting for you to manifest. You are not waiting on God. God is waiting on you. He's given you His name, His Word, His Spirit, His power. He's given you everything. What else can He give you?

Ephesians chapter 1, verse 3 says,

> 3 Blessed be the God and Father of our Lord Jesus Christ, who hath blessed us with all spiritual blessings in heavenly places in Christ:

You are blessed "with all spiritual blessings in heavenly places in Christ Jesus." If you're blessed with every spiritual blessing, wouldn't that include the anointing? Wouldn't that include power? Wouldn't that include gifts? In other words, what are you lacking? If you've been blessed with every spiritual blessing, then that means you don't need any more blessings from God.

You just need to walk them out, and then the law of sowing and reaping can kick in to where the more you give out, the more you get. Did you know that if you move 10 percent out, God will put 100 percent back in you? He's waiting on you. You're not waiting on Him.

"Well, we're just waiting on the move of God." No. Let me tell you, "I'm not waiting for a move of God. I am a move of God. Every time I move, God moves. If I lay my hands on the sick, God moves. If I lay my hands on them, God lays His hand on them." Why? It is because He is waiting for me to do it.

I'm not waiting on a move of God. You need to understand that God is waiting on you.

Many of you, for whatever reason, get burdened down with something. I heard one man say, "Do you know why we need to be filled over and over again?" He said, "Because, we leak." I can understand that.

I'm not saying I don't have times when my emotions come into play because of external circumstances. Sometimes there are things going on around me that I don't like. There's a certain amount of humanity there. There are things that I don't like, and there are people I don't like.

I'll be honest with you. I love them, but I don't like them. Even though I don't love them I would still help them if they needed help. I might not like you, but I'll still help you. Just because I help you doesn't mean I like you. It just means I love you. I've learned that there are times when your emotions can get you down.

The problem is that you tie the emotions to the power of God. You think that because your emotions are down, the power level is down. I'm telling you, "The power level is always up. The only problem is that when your emotions are down, you're not as likely to step out and do something."

That's why you've got to die to self to the point that you think in terms of, "I don't care if I just got angry at this person; God doesn't love them any less." You shouldn't have gotten angry, obviously, but do you think God loves the person that is crippled any less because you just messed up?

Are you trying to heal the sick because you're so great, or are you doing it because God loved them enough to send Jesus to bear His stripes so that He would bear their sickness? If you are messed up, it has nothing to do with the power of God. If you are messed up, it has nothing to do with God's love for that person.

Get over yourself, and don't let yourself get in the way of you doing the will of God. You've got to be able to die to that point where you don't let your emotions dictate what goes on; that is, unless you can control your emotions to the point where it doesn't matter anymore. That's the way it should be. You have to realize that God is in you, with you, and for you.

Dr. Lake said, "If you do not lay your hands upon anyone, they will not be healed, however, if you have faith to believe that you have the Holy Spirit to be used by Him and for Him, your heart and your hands will be ready. It is a sad thing to me that God has to go out on a special mission, and hunt a soul up and wrestle with him in order to get him to do something for God."

Isn't that what we always tell God? We say, "God, if You want me to do it, You move me, You lead me, and I'll do it." Did you ever realize when you were a sinner that you didn't have to be led into sin? You did it on your own. Do you know why? You were led into sin, because that was your nature. Well, if you get a new nature, shouldn't your new nature also lead you to do what is righteous? It says in 1 John 3:7, "He that does righteous is righteous."

What makes you think that the Holy Spirit should have to lead you to do anything? Do you like having to tell your kids everything they do, or do you want them to grow up and do what needs to be done, without having to be told?

We understand that, yet we turn around and make it all spiritual in the church. Do you know why we do that? It is because we don't want the responsibility that every time we see a sick person, we're supposed to do something. We'd rather say, "You know, I just didn't feel the Spirit leading me." Really? "Well, yeah, we've got to be led." Really?

Did you really check on God's leading before you planned your vacation, or did you choose where you wanted to go? Isn't that funny? You have to be led to do a good thing, but you don't have to be led to do what you want to do. Maybe you just need a little more of your nature changed into His nature, to the point where you would even look toward the cross with joy. Think about that. Amen?

Dr. Lake goes on to say, "There used to be a Bible School in Ohio where they waited in continuous prayer meeting for nine months for the gifts of the Holy Ghost. I said to them, 'It seems to me if you stay around for ten years and nine months, you will miss the gifts of the Holy Ghost, but if you take off your coat, and go out, and use what God has given you to bless others, He will give you more.'" Do you hear that? Do not wait.

People wait and tarry, and tarry and wait. It's amazing. Jesus said, "Wait," one time. He said, "Go," over and over again. One time He said wait, and the church has been waiting ever since. We don't take into account all the times He said, "Go."

Dr. Lake said that the Bible School was in a building in Finley, Ohio. Do you know what that building is today? It is a funeral home. Now, tell me that that is not prophetic.

The reason I am taking you there is because I want you to hear what John Lake said about the Holy Spirit. He said, "God gives us the Holy Ghost to use for Him." Think about that.

Before I get into Mark 16, I want to tell you a story. I was with Dr. Lester Sumrall for several years, and he was in South Bend, Indiana. In South Bend, there was a car factory where they made Studebaker, and they also made a car called Avanti. We got to go through the plant one time on a tour, to look at it, and see what it was like. While I was there, I had an amazing revelation from God. Isn't it amazing where God can give you a revelation? It can be anywhere.

I went through this factory, and in the very corner were stairs. You had to walk up all these stairs to get to a tiny room that had glass windows. As we walked up, we saw a man sitting there. This man wasn't very impressive. He wasn't a big guy. He didn't have big muscles. He was just sitting there.

As we looked out, there was this rail system. We were watching this man, and he was sitting there, and he was not even sweating. The room was air conditioned, and he was sitting there, just relaxing, and there were these joysticks sitting there.

He was just moving these joysticks around. He would tap one, move it, hold it, and turn it loose. It wasn't like he was even trying. He was just moving it: zip, zip, zip, and everything would move. This big crane would go across these rails, and then he would push a button, and this thing would, zip, and it would grab a car.

We're talking 3,000 pounds here. What's that, 1,361 kilograms? It is something like that. He would grab this thing, and pick it up, and he would push a button, and it would zip, and then he'd pull the thing back. It would zip, and raise it up. He would tap it, zip, and move it. We're talking 3,000 pounds, and this man was moving it with a finger! It was amazing!

God spoke, and He said, "That's the Holy Ghost." Do you get it? That man can't raise 3,000 pounds, but there was something between his hand and that car that amplified his intentions and will to accomplish what he was trying to do. Amen?

When I got that, I realized that God gives us the Holy Ghost just as he gave that man the crane. Can I heal the sick? No, I can't. However, between my hands and their skin, there is Someone that can, and He is called the Holy Ghost.

Unless I lay my hands on them, He can't work, because He has no body. He is a Spirit waiting for the opportunity to manifest through a body.

It is the same thing with demons. Why do you think demons want to inhabit humans? They need a body. They are a spirit, and they need a body.

The Holy Ghost is a Spirit. He needs a body. Now, the beauty of it is this: when you got born again, you were appointed, anointed, set apart, sanctified, and consecrated unto God.

Because you are sons, He sent the Spirit of His Son into your hearts crying, "Abba, Father."

"Abba, Father" means "My Father," which is actually more like the question, "What can I do for you?" Because of that, that Spirit in us cries out, "God, what can I do?" You can lay hands on the sick and because of that, He is waiting on you.

Let me ask you this, "If He is waiting on you, who is causing a move of God? Is it God or is it you?" It is you, because He won't move without you. If you refuse to move, then He can't move, unless He can find somebody else to move through.

The problem is that we've had teaching in the past that emphasizes waiting until the Spirit comes upon you. I could make you feel the Spirit, or at least what you would think would be the Spirit, by taking you through certain things. I could use worship to do it, to get you into a place, and then, by a mere suggestion, I could tell you the Holy Spirit is going to sweep through here from the East to the West. By mere suggestion, because you're in that place where you want it, you'd feel it.

If I convinced you that you had it, and you could use it, you'd go do it, and it would work for you, and you'd think, "That's when I got it." No, you had it all the time. It's just that when you finally believed you had it, you acted like it, and it started working.

The key is in Mark 16. I'm going to go back to verse 17 first, where it says, "And these signs shall follow." Notice, "…follow."

Now, look at Mark 16:19 and 20 where it says,

> 19 So then after the Lord had spoken unto them, he was received up into heaven, and sat on the right hand of God.
>
> 20 And they went forth, and preached everywhere, the Lord working with *them*, and confirming the word with signs following. Amen.

The King James says, "Working with *them*." You will notice the "*them*" is in italics, which means it's not in the Greek.

Read it without the word "*them*." God was not confirming men. He was confirming His Word. It says, "And they went forth and preached everywhere, the Lord working with and confirming the Word with signs following." Twice it says, "Signs are going to follow."

James 1:22 says,

> 22 Be ye therefore doers of the Word and not hearers only, thereby deceiving your own selves.

Who is the doer of the Word? We are the doers; we have to do. What does this Word here say to do? We're talking about healing, in particular, so let's just stick with healing. It says, "They will lay hands on the sick, and they will recover." To be a doer of the Word means that you've got to lay hands. It doesn't say that you lay hands because you see results. You can't see results until you start laying hands.

Doing the Word is not based on results. Doing the Word is based on what the Word tells you to do, so you have to do the Word, no matter what. Even if you didn't see results, would you still have to lay hands on the sick? Yes. It wouldn't be near as much fun, but you would still have to do it, because it is a command. It is not an option. Results or no results, you've got to do it.

You have to commit to do what the Word says, regardless of the outcome. Believe me; you can't see the outcome until you do it. The person can't get healed until you lay hands. Step one is to be a believer. That's you, right? Step two is to have a hand. You've got a hand. Step three is to find a sick person. That's pretty easy. Step four is for you to lay hands on the sick person.

People ask, "How do I lay hands on a person?" Just put your hand on the person. "What do I say? How do I pray?" I don't see anything in here about praying. Just lay hands. You don't have to pray. We are told to just lay hands. Do you know why we pray? It is because we're used to doing this in church, and in church, people are expected to pray, and they expect things to be a certain way.

In the grocery store, they don't know what you're going to do, and they don't know how it should be done. You can do it however you think it should be done, and you just lay hands. One way to lay hands is to shake hands. That's laying hands.

You lay hands on the sick, and once you lay hands on the sick, then what happens? They're supposed to recover, right? Before they can recover, there has to be a transfer of power. There has to be the healing part where it goes into them, but here it says, "These signs will follow." Then it said, "The Lord working with, and confirming the Word with signs following."

Signs do what? They follow. Do you hear that? They follow. They don't precede the laying on of hands. They follow. That means I've got to lay hands before there can be a sign. That means I have to be a doer of the Word before there can be a sign. First, I have to do something.

I didn't tell you at the beginning that the title of this message would be called, "Co-Workers with God." I do my part. What's my part? It is to be a believer and lay hands. God does His part. What's His part? He does the healing so that they can recover.

My part is to believe and lay hands. His part is to heal. The sick person's part is to recover. Isn't that the order? That would be the divine job descriptions. My job is to believe, and lay hands, then God heals, and because of that, the sick person can recover.

Jesus said that He would not leave you an orphan, but He would send a Comforter. The word for Comforter in the Greek is *paraklētos,* and is pronounced par-ak'-lay-tos. It means: a*n intercessor*, *consoler; advocate.* In English transliteration it literally means: *one called alongside to help.* The One that He said is to be our *Helper* is the Holy Spirit.

John 14:16 says,

> 16 And I will pray the Father, and he shall give you another Comforter, that he may abide with you for ever;

John 14:26 says,

> 26 But the Comforter, which is the Holy Ghost, whom the Father will send in my name, he shall teach you all things, and bring all things to your remembrance, whatsoever I have said unto you.

Here is the problem. We try to help God. When you try to help God, you are not in your job description. You are not God's helper. Who needs a helper? A doer needs a helper. If I'm going to do something, I might need help, but if I'm not going to do it, I don't need help. I only need help if I'm going to do it.

James 1:22 says,

> 22 Be therefore doers of the Word, not hearers only.

If I'm going to be a doer, and I can't quite accomplish it, then I have to have a helper to help me. He said He would send me a Helper. The Paraclete is the Helper.

I will give you an example. Suppose I was an electrician, and I came in here, and they told me, "We're having some problems in the electrical work." Then they would ask, "While you're here, could you do some work for us?" I would say, "Yes, I've got my assistant here."

I would come in, and I would be the certified electrician, and I would have my helper, my assistant, with me. If he was a good helper, as we went around, he would notice things I didn't notice, and he'd say, "Okay, on this side… Now, when we get to this corner… We're going to need the conduit here that goes around… We're going to need this gauge of wire… As a matter of fact, we're going to need the heavy cutters and pliers… We're going to need…," and so on.

Why would he know all of that? It is because he is a good helper. I would say, "I'm going to go to town. I'll get us some lunch, and get what we need, and when I get back, have everything ready."

When I come back in, if he's a good helper, he will have everything laid out where I need it. He will have the wire around to the side, he'll have the ladder where we're going to start, and he'll have the tool pouch with every tool we could possibly need. We would then get up to go to work.

I'm the certified electrician, and that means I actually have to do the work. The helper can't do the work. It's illegal, so I have to do the work. His job is to help me.

I climb up, and I start doing the work. If he's a good helper, when I get to an area, and I start to reach back for pliers (kind of like a doctor and a nurse working together), he will know that I'm going to need some different pliers. If he's a good helper, he has seen where I'm going, and when I reach back, he's going to put it in my hand before I ask. Do you know why? It's because he's a good helper.

The Holy Spirit knows the job, and He's looking ahead, and He knows the things that are going to come, so He'll put in my hand the tools I need at the time that I need them. I don't need them ahead of time, but as I need them, He can put them in my hand, and since they are coming from Him, I have whatever tool I could possibly need.

Could I lack anything? No, I've been blessed with every spiritual blessing. Is healing a blessing? Yes. Then I'm blessed with it. Is anointing a blessing? Yes. Then I'm blessed with it. There is no lack. How can there be lack? I have the One who is the fount of everything.

As I would go through, the helper would say, "Now, on this one you're going to need this. Okay, here you go." Why? It is because he knows me, and he would know that I would rather use a hammer than a wire cutter. You say, "To cut a wire?" Yes, believe it or not, you can smash a wire with a hammer until it breaks apart. All right, it is not the best way to do things, but if it's my preference, that's what he will do. Why? He knows my preferences. He's not the doer. He's the helper.

Different people have different kinds of gifts. That's why William Branham could be so accurate in his gifting of the word of knowledge. He didn't have the gift of healing. He had the word of knowledge, and he would share people's secrets. He would tell someone something, and he would ask, "Isn't that true?" He would then give them details.

He might tell them which town they came from, their spouse's name, their street address, what kind of car they came in, etc. By the time he would finish, the person would be standing there, just crying, because they knew God had told him this.

He would say, "Now, if God told me that about you don't you think God cares enough about you to heal you?" They would say, "Yes," and he'd say, "Go your way." Why? What did he do? He used a gift to get their faith to rise so they could grab it.

Now, is that a gift of healing? No. It's a word of knowledge, but it could be used to get somebody healed. Why? It is because, to a man with a hammer, every problem looks like a nail.

That's the way it is. You don't need to be like somebody else and get his or her gift. Just be you, and wherever you flow, whichever way works best for you, God will meet you where you work best. He can meet the needs of any person you come in contact with. He will manifest Himself through you in that way.

Paraclete means *a helper*. We're the doer, and He's the *Helper*. Who heals? The Spirit heals. We can't heal. We lay hands. The Spirit heals. Notice: "Signs follow." Step one, find the person, and lay hands on them. After you lay hands, notice the signs that are going to follow. Who's doing the signs? The Holy Spirit! I'm doing the work, and the Holy Spirit is doing the healing, but signs follow.

If I'm doing the work and He's actually causing it to happen, and healing is a sign that's going to follow, and He's doing the healing, then who is following whom? If I have to lay hands first, and a sign can't follow until after I lay hands, and the Holy Spirit is the one that heals, then it's not me following the Spirit; the Spirit is following me. Amen? Think about that.

If you get a hold of this, you'll realize that God gives you the Holy Spirit to work for Him. He gives you the crane to move the cancer, to move the HIV, or whatever it is. It is not that you could do it in and of yourself, but the beauty of it is you are not in and of yourself. It is Christ in you. "The Spirit of my Father is in me."

Do you realize that Jesus didn't even claim power? He didn't even claim it. He said, "I'm not doing these works; the Spirit of the Father in me, He does them." Well, then, shouldn't we at least be that humble so as to agree with Him, and have the same mind that was in Christ? That is to say, "It's not me doing this. It's the Spirit of my Father in me."

If it's the Spirit of my Father, then that means that I have the Spirit. That was His Spirit, the Spirit of His Son put into me whereby I can cry, "Abba, Father." We give honor and glory to God for the work done. That means that you have what you need in you.

Are you connected to Heaven? Yes. Are you connected to God? You're seated there with Him; you're connected to Him, but it's not a flow from there. It says in John 7:38,

> 38 He that believeth on me, as the scripture hath said, out of his belly shall flow rivers of living water.

In Proverbs 1:23 He said, "I will pour out my Spirit."

> 23 Turn you at my reproof: behold, I will pour out my spirit unto you, I will make known my words unto you.

If He has poured out His Spirit, it is still flowing today. There is that river that is flowing.

In Acts 2:17 He said, "I will pour out of my Spirit."

> 17 And it shall come to pass in the last days, saith God, I will pour out of my Spirit upon all flesh:

Now, think about this: as you go about, you don't have to get the person in the river; the river is in you. You may stay in the river, but the idea is being able to touch a person, and bring that river to them. That river is flowing out of you. "He will pour out of His Spirit upon all flesh." He's not touching them unless you do. Now, do you understand? For us, it's great.

Worship pumps you up, builds you up, and you get in the river of worship. It's wonderful. You're refreshed. It's good. There is nothing wrong with that; that's perfect, but when you're full, when you're blessed, and you step out, and you go to the world, they're not in the river. You've got to bring the river to them. "Out of your belly shall flow rivers of living water." You've got to go to them so that river can flow upon them.

Go with me to, Isaiah 61:1, where Jesus was quoting from:

> 1 The Spirit of the Lord God is upon me; because the Lord hath anointed me to preach good tidings unto the meek; he hath sent me to bind up the brokenhearted, to proclaim liberty to the captives, and the opening of the prison to them that are bound;

He said to proclaim liberty to the captives, not offer it to them. You don't tell them to come and get it. You proclaim it, "It's done, and you are free. I set you free." That's proclaiming, and that's what makes the difference. He says, "To proclaim liberty to the captives and the opening of the prison to them that are bound."

It goes on to say in verse 2 and 3,

> 2 To proclaim the acceptable year of the Lord, and the day of vengeance of our God; to comfort all that mourn;
>
> 3 To appoint unto them that mourn in Zion, to give unto them beauty for ashes, the oil of joy for mourning, the garment of praise for the spirit of heaviness; that they might be called trees of righteousness, the planting of the Lord, that he might be glorified.

Do you hear that? He says to comfort all that mourn. That means no mourning should go uncomforted. It says, "To appoint unto them that mourn in Zion, to give unto them beauty for ashes, the oil of joy for mourning, the garment of praise for the spirit of heaviness." He's telling you how. That's what comes upon you through the Spirit of God, through Jesus Christ, "That they might be called trees of righteousness, the planting of the Lord, that He might be glorified."

> 4 And they shall build the old wastes, they shall raise up the former desolations, and they shall repair the waste cities, the desolations of many generations.

"And they shall repair the waste cities, the desolations of many generations." That Spirit that is in Jesus, and that is in us, is to cause us to rebuild desolate places, and rebuild lives, and to rebuild cities, and to rebuild through righteousness.

I wrote an email, not too long ago, to a guy here in South Africa. I was telling him about our work, what we are doing, and how we're doing things. I told him what needed to be done and what our goals were. I said, "Imagine what would happen if this Gospel was truly preached and lived out by the people."

For one thing, hospitals would close, or be turned into churches or Bible schools. That would be fine. We wouldn't need police stations or jails. There might be some rebelliousness somewhere, but for the most part, it would be very minor.

Imagine if you can, Romans 13, where it talks about officers of the government not wielding the sword in vain. Imagine if our police departments operated in the word of knowledge. They would be there waiting for the bad guy to show up. Think about it. If they had the mind of Christ, they would know.

There is a lot of money spent on social programs, and most of that we wouldn't even need anymore. Everybody that had abundance would share. All the things that would take place would totally revolutionize this entire continent.

I was telling this guy in the email to think about this: we have the Gospel that can eradicate sickness and disease from the continent of Africa. Imagine that.

You can look at areas of Africa where crops won't grow, and we could go there and put our foot on a place, and say, "You will grow. We command you to blossom forth." It would be able to bring forth enough food to feed all of the people in Africa and start changing things.

You say, "Well, I just can't imagine that." Then you can't imagine being a manifested son of God, because Jesus, as a manifested Son of God, took a few little things, and broke them, and fed multitudes.

Imagine going into a UN center somewhere and laying your hands on sacks of rice, and the things start bursting open. Rice starts pouring out of them, and they just keep pouring out. Usually, when you open a bag, sooner or later, it stops. This doesn't. It just keeps pouring until there is more than enough. As a matter of fact, there would be so much that it could feed everybody there. They could box it, turn around, and send it to other places. Amen?

You're going to have to stretch to realize what Jesus was saying in John 14:12,

> 12 Verily, verily, I say unto you, He that believeth on me, the works that I do shall he do also; and greater works than these shall he do; because I go unto my Father.

Did He go? Yes. Then there is no excuse. We're supposed to be doing greater works. Amen?

You need to sometimes just stop, and yes, there are times when I will just stop. Sometimes, when I lay down at night to go to sleep, I'll do this. I especially do it in meetings, and a lot of times on purpose. At other times, I'll just be somewhere, and I will choose to just stop, and realize, "God walks in me. I have the Spirit of God; nothing is impossible. Nothing is too hard. With Him, all things are possible. Yes I'm with Him, so to me, all things are possible; nothing is impossible."

Impossible is beyond what you can think or imagine so that means you are to start thinking and imagining some pretty big things.

You say, "Well, do you know what? I want to get behind Spirit Word, because they're covering 80 percent of the world." Well, okay. If they've already got the 80 percent, it shouldn't be a real jump for you to jump in and help get the other 20 percent. It's not a stretch anymore.

If you really wanted to use faith, you would have had to be with them back when they were covering five percent, or ten percent. That's when you've got to stretch, and you've got to use vision and imagine things. Then you say, "We can do it. God can do it through us." That's when it takes faith.

It's amazing how people want to jump on board with you once you've already got it over the hump. All of a sudden, a person starts looking better. "Oh, yeah, we were always with you," and I say, "Yeah, I remember what you said."

You need to realize who you are and what you have. In Colossians chapter 2, verse 9, it says,

> 9 For in him dwelleth all the fulness of the Godhead bodily.

In John 1:16, it says,

> 16 And of his fulness have all we received, and grace for grace.

In John 3:34, it says,

> 34 For he whom God hath sent speaketh the words of God: for God giveth not the Spirit by measure unto him.

"And of His fullness, we have received," and "He does not give the Spirit by measure."

What makes you think He gives the Spirit in measure? That's the beauty of it. I've got all of the Spirit, and you've got all of the Spirit. You say, "How can that happen?" It's God. God's just amazing like that. He gave us Himself so that He could have a body to work through. Amen? He tells us to do this, because we're His sons.

I want my son to grow up and enjoy the things that I've seen. He's already seen the dead raised. He's already seen sickness healed. He's seen things, not just in my life, but also through his own hands when he was a missionary in Thailand.

I want him to grow up in the fullness and understand what it means to walk in the fullness of even what I've walked in, and go beyond that. Well, guess what that is? That's called the spirit of a father.

The father always wants the son to do better than he did. Your Heavenly Father is the same way. Your Heavenly Father isn't holding things back. He's saying, "Go for it. Let's revolutionize this world. Come on. Let's get the glory of the Lord to fill the earth, where everybody can say they're blessed of the Lord." Amen.

Say this with me:

"Father, I believe Your Word. You have sanctified me with Your Word, and Your Word is truth. I will live by this truth. I will obey the truth. I will walk in the truth. I will forget about me, and I will live Your life. I will manifest Your Son, and I will become a manifested Son. I will walk in the fullness. I will enjoy my life in You. I walk in power. I walk in truth. I walk in integrity. I will be dependable, because You are dependable, Father, and I am just like You, in the name of Jesus. Father, I thank You that Your Spirit is in me and that You sent Your Word, and it healed them all. I've heard Your Word. I've received Your Word, and I'm healed. I'm delivered. I'm free. As it is in Heaven, so is it in me, in the name of Jesus. Father, I will be faithful to transmit this to others who will be faithful, and this will spread like a wildfire; the fire of God, consuming everything in its path. I will be a catalyst for that fire, in the name of Jesus. So be it."

Strength to Carry On

Strength to Carry On
Messages to Strengthen Your Commitment

The Coming Revolution

The message that you have been hearing from me and from others in leadership is not just a message of reformation, as we all know. It is a message of revolution. There must be a revolution.

We can't have reformation. Russia had a reformation, and it is still in trouble. The reason it is still in trouble, is because a reformation changes the looks of things, but it doesn't change the leadership, it doesn't change the heart, or the mechanism, so Russia is still Russia. It doesn't matter what face they put on, they still have a lot of the same old cronies in positions of power.

When I'm talking about the church, I'm not talking about the church that we know as the body of Christ. I am talking about the church, visible. I'm talking about the organizations, and denominations, and the leaderships, and different things like that.

They don't mind if you preach what we have been preaching as long as you don't push it. As a matter of fact, as long as you can draw a crowd they will love you, because crowds equal money to them.

The problem comes in when you start to step over the line of boundaries they have drawn, because then you question their authority. However, it is really important that you realize that you can't just hear a message. Hearing the message is not enough. Hearing the message does not get the job done.

The Bible tells us to be renewed in the spirit of the mind. When I say that, people quote Romans 12: 1 and 2. It says, "Have your mind renewed to the Word."

> 1 I beseech you therefore, brethren, by the mercies of God, that ye present your bodies a living sacrifice, holy, acceptable unto God, which is your reasonable service.
>
> 2 And be not conformed to this world: but be ye transformed by the renewing of your mind, that ye may prove what is that good, and acceptable, and perfect, will of God.

You can have your mind renewed to the Word and still not have the spirit of your mind renewed. Ephesians 4:23 says,

> 23 And be renewed in the spirit of your mind;

That is something that I have been seeing more and more. I have people all across the country that can quote this message as good or better than I can, and a lot of them are much better preachers. They can quote it; they've got it down.

That's one of the things I have been noticing even in mainline denominations; charismatic groups that believe in healing. They can quote doctrinal healing. They can tell you what it says. They can tell you that healing is for everybody, healing is for all time, and God wants to heal.

They can quote all of that, yet most of the time, they are quoting from their intellect. They know it. They have heard it. They have heard it preached, they have read it, but the spirit of their mind has not been renewed. You can't just have the intellect.

There was a time when you thought that healing wasn't for today, but then you had your mind renewed and found out that healing is for today. Now, you have to go beyond having your mind renewed to having the spirit of your mind renewed, and when you have the spirit of your mind renewed, it is not just a doctrine; it is a way of life. It is a fact. It is your heritage. It is your birthright.

One thing I am noticing is that a lot of people have their minds renewed, but they don't have the spirit of their minds renewed. They can quote everything. They can quote the famous preachers and all of their bylines, but they have not been renewed in the spirit of their minds.

They can quote positive Scriptures. I'm not talking about just being positive minded. I am not talking about that at all. They can quote Scriptures that sound positive, and yet their spiritual countenance is not positive. You can hear it in their voices.

I am not coming in here and telling you what you are doing wrong. I'm not doing that at all. If I mention something, it is not that I'm saying you are doing it. I am just putting it out, so you'll know it and won't do it. Don't think that just because I say something that I'm trying to fix something; I'm not. God has put this on my heart, so I know what the Spirit of God is doing. I want to emphasize this.

I was up in Challis, Idaho a while back with David Hogan, Roland Baker, Bill Mercer, Kris Vallotton, and a few others. We were all preaching. At one point, while I was ministering, I asked about the music. When I got up to preach for the first time, I asked, "If someone came in that was a sinner and didn't know anything, but they were looking for God, and if they heard what we are singing, would they say, 'These people know God,' or would they say, 'These people are just like me. They are looking for God.'"

If you analyze songs, you need to make sure that what you are singing doesn't violate what you have been renewing your mind to. The only reason I am mentioning this is for this purpose: the songs we sing should be for the next move of God.

That move of God will be a revolution. Do you know what that means? That means that the entire church order will be in it. That doesn't mean that you are going to go into a church and set the leaders out on the sidewalk. That's not what I am talking about.

There has been a prophecy by someone local that tells us that a civil war is coming in the church; a splitting and parting of ways in the church.

It won't be the charismatics against the non-charismatics. That is not going to be it. It will be the religious against the free. That is where the civil war is going to be. It is going to be the religious bureaucrats, those people who find their security in religion, against people who have freedom.

Many times people honestly don't understand these things, but other times they have chosen not to participate. You can see the look on their faces. They stand around with their arms folded, and look around, and say, "That's not right." You can just see it.

The revolution that is going to come is going to be drastic. It has got to be.

Now, here is the problem. Many of you are ministers in training, and you are going through the Bible School. You are all ministers in training, regardless of what level you are, or where you are, or what you are doing. Here is the thing I am most concerned about: the most dangerous thing that can happen to you, as ministers that are ready to be launched out, is that you come here, get filled with the Word of God, get on fire for God, and then get sent out. You can be boiling hot on fire for God, but if you are put into a bowl of cold water, you will have a tendency to drop to that level.

You don't hear me use terms like "Open Heavens," often, just because we are the "Open Heavens" of God. A Christian is an "Open Heaven." We are the conduit to Heaven for the world. Wherever you go, you are the "Open Heaven." You don't have to go and find it. You are it.

Someone else may have a closed heaven, and they can't get their prayers answered, but you can bring "Open Heavens" to them and get their prayers answered.

The problem is that when you go out, you won't always be around the type of people you are around right now. Many of you have been out and have come back in, and you know what I'm talking about.

A lot of people talk about cities, saying, "This city is the worst. It has this principality or that principality." I hear that everywhere I go.

I have been told that they have the highest cancer rate or mortality rate per person in the United States. Everywhere I go people say the same thing.

Do you know what the sad part is? The Christians are the ones saying that. Christians are the ones that are putting these powers in place. The Christians are the ones saying, "We have more cancer." The devil says, "That's right, you do, and I just have your word for it," because if anybody has power in their words, it's us.

You have the world saying, "This is a bad cancer," and then you have the church saying, "Oh, yes, it's bad." Why is it bad? You are there. If it is bad, and you are there, then you aren't doing your job. It's time that you started doing your job. Amen?

I want to emphasize that I want you to get your mind renewed. You have to realize that it is not even a matter of us saying, "Lord, we are going to take that hill." God is going to say, "When are you going to take it? I have already given it to you."

We are not trying to fight up the hill, trying to keep the devil off. We've got the hill. Our job is just to keep the garden.

I agree in aggressive warfare in spiritual things. I agree in going after things, but at the same time, we have to realize that we are fighting from a position of power. We are fighting from a position of victory already, so when we walk in, sickness and disease should be an affront to us. "How dare that thing think that it could attack that person's body, in here, among us? That thing has some kind of gall to think it is going to get away with it."

First, it was a dumb spirit to think that it was going to get away with it. Amen? How would you like to come into a meeting like this knowing that your job was to steal, kill and destroy knowing that there is a lot of life running all around you, just waiting to swallow you up?

That is who we are. Every time we shake hands, life ought to be imparted. Every time we speak a word, life should be imparted, because the words are Spirit and life. The Word says, "There is life, and there is Spirit."

I want you to understand that you are not who you think you are. I have said this before, and like Paul said, "It is not grievous for me to come, because instead of writing to you, I get to speak to you, again." That's even better.

Some people don't like my style of preaching They say that I should speak with grace, and let everything edify the hearer, and I agree. My response is that I would love to preach like E. W. Kenyon writes.

Kenyon says things like, "Now, you understand why this is. Now, you get this," as opposed to an aggressive, almost a negative type of preaching that I have had to do. I have had to preach in an aggressive manner, because a lot of times, when I go into places, I have to attack strongholds. I can't walk in, and say, "Now, you see," because they don't see, so I have to go in and actually blast these things, and go against them.

The response I generally get is an emotional response from people. They think I am mean, because I am not the typical preacher. I don't go in, and say, "Everything is going to be okay." Maybe I don't look at the camera just right.

I want to get across to you that this is life and death. We think sometimes that this is easy. We bring people up, and pray for them, and then go on about our business. I don't want to see anyone else die.

When you go to pray for someone and minister to them, you cannot pray out of pity, because pity isn't faith. You can't pray out of fear. You can't have a knee-jerk response. That is not what you do.

One of the instances I had one time is I realized that after I prayed, the devil tried to convince me that I had not done enough. He tried to get me to do something else, and I had to realize that there was a positive faith movement that I could do after praying. There are things you can do, and that's fine, but there is also a negative fear based thing based on "I am not done yet, because I haven't done enough."

I'm not talking about praying for someone over and over again. That's exactly right, and you should do that. The difference is, I don't pray for people over and over again based on how I did it last time, thinking, "Maybe I didn't do it well enough or maybe I didn't do it right."

When you do that, you go in thinking you are starting all over again. That is not what I do. Every time I go back and lay hands, I am not starting over. I am just adding to. I am not coming into it based on a point of view, "What if I didn't do something right? What if I didn't do it enough? What if I didn't say it just right?" You can't pray that way.

You have to go out, and say, "Look, I put in all I had, and the next time I get to put hands on, I will do it again." We will keep adding on bricks to this wall until we have a wall built big enough to stand between whoever we are praying for and the devil that's after them. We will just keep putting life into them, and adding life to them, until life abounds. That is the point we have to get to.

If you're sick, don't take this as any kind of condemnation. I hope you know me well enough to know that that is not my heart. I am just trying to raise the bar a little, so we will quit coming up for prayer, getting healed, going back and getting sick, coming back and getting healed, and going back and forth.

That is not God's will. God's will is for us to get well, stay well, live in divine health, and take our abundance of health to other people.

I agree wholeheartedly with something that E. W. Kenyon said, "The message of righteousness is the most important message ever offered to the church." I believe it, because the church still doesn't understand it. For lack of a better term, we are double minded. We talk a good fight, and we give a good pep rally, but when it gets down to it, we end up collapsing.

As a last resort, you say, "We don't know what else will work, so we are just going to get down on our face and beg God." That is not who you are. I am not saying that there isn't a place for it. There is a time and place, and there are circumstances. There are rules, and there are laws of prayer.

It is like playing sports. There are rules for every sport. You don't play soccer by baseball rules. There are different types of prayer and different rules for praying different ways. If you try to pray one type of prayer and pray it with another type of prayer's rules, it won't work. You have to get things lined up. I am not talking about being so specific that you have to walk a thin line. It is very simple.

If you get the idea of righteousness and who you are, all of that gets cleared up, because now you no longer try to walk a tightrope. You are just being who you are. Whatever you say will bring life, because that's who you are. You are life. In 2 Corinthians 6:15, it says,

> 15 And what concord hath Christ with Belial? or what part hath he that believeth with an infidel?

Guess who He is likening that to? That is you. You are the light, and then there is darkness. He is saying, "Don't hang out with it." There is a contrast.

I would like for you to go back, and read Romans, chapters 1 through 7. I like to give a background and not start in the middle of something, but for the sake of time, we are going to start with Romans chapter 8, verse 1,

> 1 There is therefore now no condemnation to them which are in Christ Jesus, who walk not after the flesh, but after the Spirit.

Depending on which text you use, that last part, "…who walk not after the flesh, but after the Spirit," is either in the Greek text, or it's not. It doesn't matter if it is there or not. If you are in Christ, you aren't going to walk after the flesh. Verse 2 says,

> 2 For the law of the Spirit of life in Christ Jesus hath made me free from the law of sin and death.

We are going to talk about sin, sickness, and physiology, and how it works together. If you try to drive down the road with your emergency brake on, your car will go on down the road to some degree. The power of the engine will overrule the brakes, and it will burn up your brakes.

Most Christians are doing that same thing, especially Spirit filled, charismatic, Bible believing Christians. They are probably worse about it than anyone else, mainly because they say, "God is able, God can, and God wants to," but when they go to pray for someone, there is always that "What if," or they say, "What about this time? I am not sure about this time." As you minister to people, you are going to be bringing life out of you.

Maybe you had never been in church in your life before Jesus found you, and you didn't know anything about the Bible, but it didn't matter. You may not have known anything about the

Bible, but you knew something about religion. Because of our society, there is religion all around us to some degree. As long as you don't step over the boundaries that religion has set, you are okay.

If there is going to be a true revolution, the revolution is stepping over the boundaries. That's it. In Tiananmen Square, when that one person stood in front of that tank, he was stepping over the boundaries. It was so funny to watch that tank try to go around him. He would just step over, and that tank would back up. Imagine the power in that tank, and he stopped it there. That was the first step.

In a revolution, there has to be a total wiping out of the old and a total re-institution of what was supposed to be there. That's what is coming. In order for that to happen, you are going to have to step over the mental barriers that religion has put in you. That is why you have to be renewed in the spirit of your mind. That is the whole point.

Those of us who are mature, but who are still young in heart and mind, have an advantage over those who are still young. That advantage is that we get to a point where we don't really care what people say, and we are willing to try unusual things. We really don't care as long as we think we are right.

The problem is you have to get out into the world. You have been trained, and you are on fire. You get out there, and there is this group that is going to say, "Yes, we heard good things about a certain Bible school."

While you are attending that Bible school, they will tell you, "Let's do this," and you say, "I can't do that, because this is where I am, and this is where I am going, and this is what God has put on my heart." They say, "That's alright. It is good that you can do that, but help us with this, and we can help you with that."

I am not telling you to be segregated and not working with anybody. I am not telling you to be that way, but don't compromise. Do not allow them to draw you in.

They aren't going to walk up, and say, "Turn away from this, and go to this." They don't say, "Jump over here." They won't do that. They will draw you in, step by step.

They will water you down, and they will try to dilute you until you are no different than they are. Then, they will love you, because you aren't putting pressure on them anymore; you aren't making changes anymore. They will start saying things like: "We can help you with this. You don't realize what we can do for you." When you hear those words, run.

It is not them putting you anywhere. God will put you where He wants you to be. I could not put myself in the place I am in. God has done it. I am still trying to figure out how He did it, but He just keeps doing it.

The reason I am telling you this is because I have experienced it. I have seen what they try to do. The bad part is that you never realize it when they are telling you that. You only realize it once you have made two steps toward them.

Strength to Carry On

You look back, and think, "Wait, where am I?" The first time they say something and expect you to agree and you want to agree, even though you don't believe that way, that is the danger sign.

If you want to be a part of a revolution, get ready, because it is going to be like nothing you have ever experienced. You are not going to be liked.

Right now, people like you; they've heard good things. If you will do your job, for the most part, that will cease. Do you know why a lot of people like you? It is because you are here.

Go to their town, and they may not like you, because you will be a threat. You will be a threat against their numbers, because they will be afraid you will steal their people. You will be a threat against their money, because if you get their people, you get their money.

You will be a threat against their position, because if you come in and start getting results and they aren't, people are going to look at you differently than they do them, and it is going to lower them in the eyes of their people.

The reason I am saying this is because you have to get grounded in who you are in Christ and who He is in you, and when you do that, you won't care what people think. Like I have said before, I get invited to a lot of places one time, and that is fine with me, because I have to go into all the world anyway, so that is just one more place I have already been.

I want people to like me, but at the same time, I have One that has to like me, and I have to make sure that He likes me whether anyone else does or not. I have to preach what I see in the Word, and I am going to have to live by that, because I am going to have to answer for it.

We aren't here to just set up a building, a church, and a system. We are here to change the world. Let me ask you this, "When you go back to where you were before the school, or if you go to a new place, are people going to say about you what they said about the early Christians? People said about the early Christians, "These people that are turning the world upside down have now come here, also."

Do you know which world they were turning upside down? They were turning the religious world upside down. They weren't turning the community upside down. They weren't telling the people to quit their jobs and close down their shops. They came in and turned the religious world upside down.

When you come into town, are you going to turn the religious world upside down? Are you going to put pressure on the religious devils that have begun to inhabit the religious leaders? The first thing the devil wants to do is get a hold of religion, economics, and politics. If he can get a foothold in those three areas, then he pretty much has everything wrapped up. Now, you can even see where he has started to blend those things in together.

There is a law of the Spirit of life in Christ Jesus. Who are you in this law? You are life. He is in you and you are in Him. He is life so you are life. He said, "I am the Light of the world," and then turned around, and said, "You are the light of the world."

Religion has built this thing up that says, "You don't want to step across that line." You ask, "What is that line?" That line is your identification in Christ. The moment that you begin to talk like Jesus did, and as soon as you begin to do the things Jesus did, you will begin to get persecuted.

Do you realize the only people the devil never blasted were the religious people? Those are the only ones. There is a seducing spirit that will try to get you to not speak out against this thing or that thing, because this spirit wants you to conform to it. It wants to keep control of the people.

We aren't here to control people. We are here to help people and to lift people. Religion will always keep people codependent, but Jesus frees people and makes us all interdependent.

Which one are you? Are you codependent or interdependent? One might say, "I just want to make sure my salary is secure, and after I have preached 30 or 40 years, then I can retire." That is not what Christianity is about. First of all, people look at ministers as someone special. I have always considered myself different but not special. I don't do anything that I know of by a gift, although I believe that God has gifted me.

I do what I do as a Christian, laying hands on the sick, ministering to the sick, and casting out devils. That is Christian work. That is not minister work. That is Christian work, and you do that whether you have a business card with your ministry name on it or not. You have to reach the point where you do that automatically, and then going from that, depending on your gifts, and how God is using you, then God can place you in certain positions doing certain things.

You are going to have to differentiate between your ministry and your relationship with God. They are interrelated, but if you relate the two totally together, then as long as people come to your meetings, and your offerings are up, and you are booked securely, you will kick back, and say, "Things are going pretty good." That is the lie, because that doesn't mean things are going good.

There is a secular saying that I don't like all the wording in, but I am going to go ahead, and quote it, "Who the gods wish to destroy, they first make rich." We know, of course, there is only one God, and He doesn't wish to destroy you. It is the god of this world who is trying to destroy you. The Bible says, "The blessings of the Lord make us rich and add no sorrow," so we know that the secular saying doesn't apply to Christians.

There is one thing I do know. The same devil that made up that saying will try to get you to live by it. He will try to get you comfortable. He will try to get you in a secure place. He will try to get a ministry built up, and he will try to get you into a place that will make you think everything is going good. He will get you into a place, so you can kick back. It is like you just push in the clutch, and just coast, spiritually, because you can preach, you can pray, and you can do everything you need to do.

When you pray, you can pray with unction; with push. You can do that but does your life have push behind it, or are you just comfortable? Do you only have push when you are preaching?

That's what the devil tries to do. He has tried to do that with me and everybody else I ever talked to that preaches.

We aren't here just for preaching. We are here to change the world. Jesus changed the world with twelve men. We have a room full here. What should we be able to do? If what we have is what we claim, what is our potential here?

You think, "Who am I?" I will tell you who you are. You are the person that Jesus thought about when He was on the cross. You are the one He died for. You are the one He put His Spirit in so that He could live again on this earth and show Himself strong, through you. That's who you are. You are a person that was born by the Spirit of God. You are not even the same person, obviously, that you were before you got born again.

Let's go to Hebrews, chapter 11. This is amazing. You think you have heard it all preached, but the more I read here in Hebrews, it just keeps coming out more and more. It talks about all of the things that they went through.

If half the ministries were going through the sufferings listed in Hebrews 11, people would look at them, and say, "What's wrong with them? They must have missed God. God must have left them."

Hebrews 11:33 and 34 says,

> 33 Who through faith subdued kingdoms, wrought righteousness, obtained promises, stopped the mouths of lions,

> 34 Quenched the violence of fire, escaped the edge of the sword, out of weakness were made strong, waxed valiant in fight, turned to flight the armies of the aliens.

In verse 34, it says that they "quenched the violence of fire, and escaped the edge of the sword." In verse 33, it says, "Who through faith subdued kingdoms."

Mary, Queen of Scots, said that she feared the prayers of one man, John Knox, more than she did all of the armies that sailed. Now, think about that. I would say that He subdued a kingdom; just by faith.

It says, "They wrought righteousness (by faith), obtained promises, and stopped the mouths of lions." We get all worked up anytime anything goes wrong. We ask, "Why is this happening? I must have messed up." No! This is called life.

We live in a world that has sin it. We live in a world where there is an enemy who is against us, and he would like nothing better than to kill us off before we can open our mouths.

We have to realize that this world is not who we are. We don't even belong here, but we keep living like we do. We keep planning like we belong here.

I have never had anyone tell me, "Brother Curry, the things you taught me don't work." I have never had that to happen. I have had people tell me, "I can get this to work and that to work, but I can't get this other thing to work for some reason." I have had that happen.

After I talk to them for a little while, I find out that it is the emergency brake thing; every time. I have heard them say, "I believed God for this. I sure am glad I didn't put all of my eggs in one basket, because it didn't come through." Maybe it didn't come through because you *didn't* put all of your eggs in one basket. That is that emergency brake.

We sing about total abandonment to God. We talk about it, we preach about it, but are we totally abandoned to God? In other words, what emergency brakes do we have? What safety catches do we have? What securities do we have?

If you are saying, "I believe for this, but I can always do something else," you can stop right there. You might as well go and do the other thing because you are not in faith. All you are doing is putting a black eye on people that are trying to live by faith. You are going to go around and talk about how God has failed you. You wouldn't say that, but you would talk about it anyway, and you would say something similar to that.

God has never failed faith. God has never failed one person. He has never shown up too late for one person in faith. We have to realize what the Bible says in Colossians 1:27, "Christ in you, the hope of glory."

Hebrews 11:35 says,

> 35 Women received their dead raised to life again…

Women had their dead raised to life, and they didn't even rate being named. Do you see that? There are only two women named in Hebrews 11; Sarah the mother of faith and Rahab the harlot. Do you know why they put those two in there? They were put in for the spectrum of humanity, to show that somewhere in between those two, you are there. You can always fit in. The next part of verse 35 says,

> 35 ...and others were tortured, not accepting deliverance;

They turned it down. It doesn't say that deliverance wasn't offered. The Scripture says that they turned it down, "not accepting deliverance." This is an entirely different mindset. When you go to a different country, like Saudi Arabia, and stand on a street corner, and put up a sign that says, "Jesus is Lord," you will probably stir up a little commotion.

We automatically think, "I will be a martyr for Christ." That could be. Some are; no doubt about it. By all natural means, that's true, but I am telling you that there could come a place where you could do that same thing, and you could walk right through the midst of them, and they couldn't touch you.

I am saying, "Go in there with the idea that you are willing to die for the Gospel, but don't go in planning to die. Plan to live through it supernaturally." We all should have that mindset before we go anywhere. You should have that mindset before you get out of bed. You should be willing to die for the Gospel.

Once you get the fear of death out of you, nobody can stop you. If you get fear out of you, nothing can stop you. I would almost say that faith is the absence of fear, and I don't mean not feeling, because you can have the feeling. You just don't listen. You can have all kinds of people talking to you; you just don't listen. Christians can tell you what you can't do. Faith keeps on walking and goes and does it while the others stand there telling you that you can't do it.

People in the leadership here have probably been told that they can't do this school, because it won't work. I have heard all kinds of things. I have been to churches, and people have told me, "We are under a curse." The first thing I say is, "Who cursed you?" "We were birthed out of a church split, and since we were the group that lost the building, we were the ones that were cursed because we left." "Show me that in the Bible. Are you still in the body of Christ?" "Yes." "Then you aren't cursed. How can Christ curse Himself?"

Where is the curse going to come from? It won't come from God. The Bible says that Jesus became a curse for us. He didn't make a curse on us. You can't curse me. I pity you if you do. It won't ever reach me. You are just throwing a boomerang. That's all you're doing. I have my shield of faith, and it quenches every fiery dart. Half of the time, I don't even know about it.

I don't know how many things that God has healed me of that I never even knew I had. I wake up every day, and mercy is new every day. Healing is mercy, so I get healed every day. If the devil comes in and tries to hit me with something, then it heals before I even know about it. Why? I am healed, because "I walk in the shadow of the Almighty. Even though I can see to my left and to my right, it won't come near me, and it won't come near my dwelling." We are not those who have no hope. The rest of verse 35 says,

> 35 ...that they might obtain a better resurrection:

Hebrews 11:36 and 37:

> 36 And others had trial of cruel mockings and scourgings, yea, moreover of bonds and imprisonment:

> 37 They were stoned, they were sawn asunder, were tempted, were slain with the sword: they wandered about in sheepskins and goatskins; being destitute, afflicted, tormented;

These were people in faith. There are some groups that would start cursing you if you were put in any of those positions, and they would say, "Oh, look! You are doing something wrong," and you might not have done anything wrong.

If someone heard that my vehicle broke down, they would automatically say, "What did you do wrong?" "I'm not a mechanic. I didn't check it. I just heard it. When it started making a noise, I stopped as soon as I recognized what it was doing." That doesn't mean I did anything wrong.

Jesus said, "Do you think these Galileans were any worse than anybody else?" We automatically have a theology that if something bad happens to us, it must be God. "We must be out of God's will." You are all just like Job. You are always saying, "What did I do wrong?"

Job has been maligned, because it is seen as a negative book, but it is a positive book. It is not a negative book. You should stand that strong through all persecution with everyone coming at you all the time and saying all those things to you. His own wife said, "Curse God, and die." The man was under some pressure, don't you think? I guarantee you that she didn't just say it one time. I promise you; it wasn't just once. Look at what he says in Hebrews 11:38. I have said all of that to get to this point:

> 38 (Of whom the world was not worthy:)...

All of these people are not worthy. Even Paul said, "I consider myself, as an apostle, the off-scouring," in other words, "the scum." He said, "God has made us, as apostles, a spectacle in front of people, something to be looked at, and in some cases, laughed at, and mocked and talked bad about, and persecuted with people saying, 'Where is your God now? You must have done something wrong. Look at you.'" Nevertheless, he was saying, "God has not forsaken me." Look at everything he went through.

You need to realize that you can go through these things. The faith was that they went through them, and they didn't stop in the middle of them. They didn't throw up their hands, and say, "That's it. This doesn't work. Toss the Book." Half of them didn't have a Book. They were writing the Book as they went along, and yet we think we have to have chapter and verse for every detail on every little thing.

We don't always have chapter and verse. Sometimes we just have to say, "My heart is right with God, and I am going on. That's all I know." "Why did this happen?" "I don't know." They say, "How can you trust a God that allows that to happen?" "It is because He is God, and I am not. I don't know everything that God knows. If I need to know and it is wisdom, then I will find it. He will tell me if I need to know."

You need to realize who you are. God is not against you. God is for you. If God be for you, who can be against you, successfully? Nobody can. Can sickness and disease be against you? No, it can't. Nothing can stand against you. Isn't that what God told Moses?

God told Joshua, "As I was with Moses, I will be with you. No man will be able to stand before you all the days of your life."

We are not to fight men. Our enemies are sickness, disease, sin, and demonic attacks. He said that these things can't stand against you. The problem, again, is stepping across that line.

You have to get away from the idea that you are one of the disciples. Now, you should be a disciple, but when we say disciple, we always look back in the Bible at the 12 or the 70. That is not who you are. Those men weren't born again. Do you get that? They weren't born again at that point. You need to look at what they did.

You never see them talking the same way after the Day of Pentecost. After that, did they pray? Sure they prayed. What was the one time they prayed and asked God to do anything? In Acts 4:30, they asked God to stretch forth His hands to show them signs and wonders. They didn't pray it again. Do you know what they did? They went out and performed signs and wonders.

You need to realize that you are not in the position of someone who is trying to get God to do something. God is in you, living in you. God is empowering you to do what He has told you to do.

The amazing thing is that He has even told you that you can do what He hasn't told you to do. It is amazing! "Yeah, but you don't know me and my problems." No, but I know Jesus, and I know that His righteousness overrules your unrighteousness. That is why it says it is the Name of Jesus and faith in His Name. Do you have faith in His Name? If you do, then you are in.

You don't have to be perfect and have everything just right. That is the beauty of this thing. He said, "Be perfect for I am perfect." Be mature. Be complete. Be right. Do you realize that your idea of perfect and the idea of perfect in the person sitting next to you are two different things? You could be perfect in your own eyes, and your neighbor would say you aren't perfect. Actually, it is more likely that your neighbor thinks your perfect, and you know you're not.

The Bible says, "We are complete in Him. His fullness we have received." He lives in you. He doesn't want you to be just another person walking around town. He doesn't want you to ask someone, "Can I tell you about Jesus?" No, don't tell them about Jesus. Show them Jesus. Be Jesus to them.

I had a poster, a few years back, on my door that said, "You may be the only Jesus some people ever see." You need to realize that He is in you. He wants to live in your body, and He wants to live through your body. "But, I work a regular job." That is fine. Then do what Jesus would do at that job. "Well, I would like to, but I can't see Jesus doing that."

If Jesus had to work the job that you are working, and somebody there was sick, He would pray for them. He would minister healing, and they would get well. "If I did that, I would get fired." Jesus would pray for them and get fired. Jesus would do it, because to not do it is the fear of man, and the fear of man brings a snare, because once it starts, it doesn't stop. It will keep boxing you in. You can do what this Book tells you that you can do. Ephesians 4:21-24 says,

> 21 If so be that ye have heard him, and have been taught by him, as the truth is in Jesus:
>
> 22 That ye put off concerning the former conversation the old man, which is corrupt according to the deceitful lusts;
>
> 23 And be renewed in the spirit of your mind;
>
> 24 And that ye put on the new man, which after God is created in righteousness and true holiness.

"And put on the new man, which after God…" Do you get that? It is saying, "The new man is created after God in righteousness and true holiness."

When you were recreated, God put in you His Spirit; His essence, and Who He is. He put that in you and recreated you in that likeness. That is why you are complete in Him. You need to realize that when you step out. God told Moses, "You are going to be as god to these people."

The problem that has been, throughout history, is that every time somebody gets a hold of this truth and starts to walk like God would walk, they get seduced; usually by a person. A person comes along beside them and begins to whisper in their ear, saying, "You are special. You are great. You are highly anointed. I think you might be Elijah. I think you might be one of the two witnesses." They might as well also be telling them, "I think you are the Antichrist," because it doesn't make any difference.

You need to realize that none of us are special. The only special One died two thousand years ago, was buried, resurrected, and now, He lives in every person that is born again. The only thing that makes us special is Him, in us. It is not us. We are nothing. We are expendable.

In the military, they used to call it cannon fodder. That is where they sent out a bunch of people, and hopefully, by numbers, they would overwhelm the enemy. They could afford to lose about 80 percent of their people. I don't know if you know it or not, but that was the entire Soviet philosophy for battle in World War II. It was just to overwhelm the Nazis with numbers, and it worked.

On one hand, it is amazing what God says about you. You are the apple of His eye. You are His heartbeat. There is not a day that goes by that He doesn't think about you. It is amazing, because when you were in sin, He loved you so much that He sent Jesus and gave up His Son for you. Now, He has you in the palm of His hands.

As dirty as you were and as bad as you were, now you are now the cream of the crop. You are precious to Him. He has cleaned you up. He has made you righteous. He has put Himself in you. You are just everything to Him.

You are looking at that part, and that is what you hear in church. You hear, "God loves you. You are the apple of His eye." You hear all of that. That is right.

On the other hand, unfortunately, what they don't tell you is that God says, "Now, you are expendable, so go out there, and win more. Go." Does He still love you? Yes, but He isn't worried about you anymore. There are people out there that are going to die and go to hell. If you die, you are not going to hell, so you are expendable.

If you will get that expendable mindset, everything will change, because you won't care anymore. How can somebody threaten you? So what! I have had knives, guns, and all kinds of things pulled on me, and I can tell you, as God is my witness, I have never had one ounce of fear of what would happen to me if they pulled the trigger or if they tried to kill me.

I don't understand it, but I can say what George Whitfield said, "Until I can complete my ministry, my mission, I am invincible." The only problem with that is you don't always know when you have completed your ministry but if you will stay ready, it won't matter.

Stay ready. Don't think you are going to get ready because you are going to figure it out, then run and get ready. Work now. Be ready. Live ready. Be who you are.

Here's what I am trying to get across to you: let Christ be formed in you until you measure up to His stature. You say, "I don't think I could ever measure up to Christ." Then you are not in the church, because it says, in Ephesians 4:13 that you are going to.

> 13 Till we all come in the unity of the faith, and of the knowledge of the Son of God, unto a perfect man, unto the measure of the stature of the fulness of Christ:

The job of the Five-Fold Ministry is to grow you up "unto that measure." That's who you are. Do you realize that until you are doing that, you are not grown?

There are some things that God has been doing lately, even in the teaching of the DHT, that have taken some major changes. It is amazing to see what God wants to do through people. The hardest people He has to convince about what He wants to do are the people He is doing it through.

You were not called to be just another person. You weren't saved just so God could put a stamp on you and say, "Okay, you get to go to heaven now." That's not who you are.

We are formed, with Christ in us so that when we speak, our words will come to pass. You ask, "Do you believe that kind of thing?" Yes, because I believe that if I speak His words they will come to pass. My job is to just make sure that my words are His words.

If you get a hold of that, then you will understand that when you put your hands on someone, you are putting His hands on them. That's because He doesn't have physical hands to put on them. That's why He told you to go, and do it. He needs us to do our job.

The Coming Revolution

I love the reality of the community that you have here. I have never had this. It has not been by choice, necessarily, but I have been on my own a whole lot. That is probably why I love coming back so much. I have not had that fellowship of peers around me, and people that I can fellowship with and talk to.

There are only two people I have ever had like that at all. One of them is still around me, thank God, but the other one I haven't seen in 20 years. There are prophetic people that speak into my life from time to time with a word that is accurate, and I accept them.

I have been in churches before, but I've never had the sense of community where it is almost like each one is equal and working together. It was always a hierarchy, and it was church. That's why I like coming here so much and being around you as much as I can.

What's coming out of that is that you are all a part of the body of Christ. If we truly believe that we are cells in the body of Christ, then when we have one cell in the body that is sick, then the whole body is sick. Isn't that what Corinthians tells us?

What are we supposed to do when there is someone sick in our midst? Are we supposed to fast? I am not saying not to fast, but we can't put our faith in that. When I say that I am going to do this for that, then automatically, it becomes a manipulation. I am not saying don't do it. We can do that; we are supposed to do that. That Bible says that Jesus said that when He was gone, his disciples would fast, so yes, you should. Just don't make it a manipulation. At the same time, as a part of the body, there is a cell that needs healing.

If your immune system is strong, then one cell in your body is not a big deal. Understand that I am not trying to belittle a sickness in a person to any degree. I understand the seriousness of it, believe me. I deal with it every day, so I understand that. I am just trying to give you God's perspective of it. A strong, healthy body should repel one sick cell. The life in the other cells will come to the aid of the one sick cell. It is not a matter of who has power, and who can pray. No. It is the body that brings life.

If you would purposely begin to emanate life all the time, then, for the most part in a church service, we wouldn't even have to lay hands on the sick. That's because of the emanation of life. Just being around Christians who emanate life should bring life.

There is really not any record, in the church, of people praying for the sick, and people getting healed in the church. What about James when he said, "If there are any sick among you?" It wasn't in the church. Now, it was in the church body, but notice that they didn't come to the church to get prayed for.

If there were any sick among them, they called for the church elders. They went to their homes and prayed for them, and then went back to church. We are not even supposed to be having healing services for Christians. We are supposed to be the healers.

That is the paradigm shift that has to take place. We have to quit seeing ourselves as battling, even though we battle. We have to see ourselves, not just as generals and soldiers, but as generals across the board.

A general doesn't say, "Well, when I tell that soldier to do something, I hope I have enough faith to enforce it." No, he doesn't say that. He knows he has been given a rank, and he might not even agree with his rank, but he submits himself to the will of the government, and says, "Well, my government knows what they are doing. This is my rank, and with my rank comes this authority so that if I speak to this soldier and tell him to do something, he will do it." Jesus spoke to a Centurion soldier and told him that his faith was the greatest faith He had ever seen.

I try not to go overboard on the military things, because it would be really easy for me to do that. I am constantly asking God, "Show me. Don't let me go too far with it," but at the same time, there is an aspect there. You, as Christians and soldiers for Christ, as the Bible says, are to suffer hardness as good soldiers. What comes with that? You have an authority that comes with that, and your authority is that you have an authority to act as an ambassador from another place.

Do you realize that if you were an E-1, no stripe private, the lowest inducted soldier and had just gone through basic, and you were brand new, and you made a landing on some island to take it over, and all of those in your unit were killed except you, do you realize that you would be the highest ranking authority on that island until someone else came along with more authority?

You, as a Christian, have the highest authority anywhere you go, because every other spirit being was created below you. I talked to a man recently who told me about a meeting where angels were showing up. He said that he would tell someone where an angel was standing, and they would go over there and stand, and they would get zapped and fall down.

He was using that to impress me with how spiritual their meetings were. He impressed me all right; just not the way he wanted to. My response back was: "The angels are there, because we are there." We don't find out where an angel is and flock to it. Angels flock to where we are. Don't you know you are going to judge angels?

In 1 Peter 1:12, it says,

> 12 Unto whom it was revealed, that not unto themselves, but unto us they did minister the things, which are now reported unto you by them that have preached the gospel unto you with the Holy Ghost sent down from heaven; which things the angels desire to look into.

Angels desire to know the things that you are hearing. They desire to know these things.

Jesus said that the greatest prophet that ever lived was John the Baptist, and yet the least in the kingdom of God is greater than him. I don't care if you are the least; you are still greater than the greatest prophet that was ever born of women. You say, "I don't believe that." I am here to tell you that it is true. I have to get this into you.

There are two reasons that most Christians don't walk in what I am talking about. Number one is: they don't ever start, because they don't believe they can handle it, or they don't believe God intended it. Number two is: they start to walk in it, and those voices will come around them and tell them how great they are, and they will succumb to pride. Those are the devil's tactics. That is what he has used all along. He will either hold you back or push you forward, but he doesn't want you to just walk.

You need to realize that when you walk into a room, and if you are the only Christian there, then you are the highest ranking spiritual authority in the room. That means that every demon, sickness, disease, sin, affliction, addiction, or anything else, has to bow. That is with one person.

We know that the Old Covenant Scriptures said that one can put a thousand to flight and with two, ten thousand. I always hear people say, "Individually, we are nothing." Well, if one can put a thousand, then that doesn't sound like "nothing" to me. It would be good enough just to be the one.

If one can put a thousand to flight and with two, ten thousand, why do we always act like the roof is going to fall in? Why do we always act like we don't believe even the very songs we sing? We sing, "Our God is an awesome God, He reigns from Heaven above." How does he reign? He reigns through us. Even our prayers say, "Thy Kingdom <u>come</u>, Thy will be <u>done</u>, on earth as it is in Heaven."

Why do we always act like we can't do anything unless there are thousands of us coming together in agreement? One Christian is stronger than any devil.

Strength to Carry On

Strength to Carry On
Messages to Strengthen Your Commitment

The Secret to Constant Victory

David Hogan and I have struck up a friendship, and I am very guarded about it. During one meeting he said, "Now, Brother Curry, this is how you stop a plague, and if a flood comes in, this is how you stop a flood," and he showed us how to do it. He believes God. I took notes as he went through different things. He said, "God told me this afternoon to give you the secret." I said, "Okay, what is it?" God knows I won't keep my mouth shut. If he tells me a secret, I will blab it all over the country.

There was a song out several years ago by Steven Curtis Chapman called, "I Will Not Go Quietly," and that is my song. It is a good song. He keeps saying, "The heart of the one who is speaking is not as true as the one he is speaking about." We are all striving toward measuring up. There is nothing wrong with living holy, but you don't get saved because of it. You live holy because you are saved. That is one part of your worship to God. He gave your life back to you. He gave you a new start in life.

Everything you do is your worship to Him. Everything you do sends up a fragrance or an odor. Your life will either be a fragrance or an odor to God. He gave our life back to us. He said, at one point that the blood of the people cried out because of the evil done to them.

One of the biggest problems in churches is that we don't live for eternity. We live for tomorrow. People tell me, "I can't think about eternity; I am trying to get my needs met today." There are two parts to that. The first thing is: when you put your eyes on eternity today, then tomorrow will take care of itself. The second thing is: when you start giving your life for others and you make others your life, then your health and your life is taken care of, because when you start taking care of others, God will take care of you.

Have you ever noticed that when you have a headache, you sit around and think about it, but if you read a book or do something, you forget about it, and it goes away? Your life will expand if you get your mind off of you. That is the true difference between saints and sinners. Sinners are always thinking about themselves. The one thing you will always hear come out of their mouth is I or me. Saints have something that makes them different from sinners, and that is: they are not focused on themselves. They are not selfish. They give their lives for others.

Is that the secret? No, that is not the secret. That is leading you into it. The secret is simple, but it requires action. That is one of the reasons people don't want to do it, because they want things handed to them. They don't want to have to do it. God gave us salvation. Notice that salvation by itself is not victory. People that are saved are going to heaven, but on their way to heaven, some saints go through hell. Salvation, in and of itself, does not guarantee you victory. It does not make you free of battle. I am going to tell you what the secret is.

"Nobody ever defended anything successfully. There is only attack and attack and attack some more." General George S. Patton, Jr.

The Secret to Constant Victory

General George S. Patton was, in my opinion, one of the greatest generals America ever produced. He was also the most feared by the Nazis, and he was the most respected. There were a lot of good generals. Eisenhower was a good general. He had the tactics and the logistics, and he could hold things together.

Joshua Lawrence Chamberlain commanded the 20th Maine Infantry of the Union forces during the Civil War at Little Round Top. The confederate forces were coming at them. His soldiers had fought so long that they literally ran out of ammunition. He gave the order to fight with bayonets, and his soldiers drove the enemy back and took captive over four hundred prisoners.

Before Chamberlain was an officer in the military, he was a school teacher. Before the soldiers wore uniforms and were trained as soldiers, they worked as something else. They were plumbers, teachers, etc. What does that have to do with this? Most of you have grasshopper vision. You think, "I am not a warrior. I am not a fighter. I don't have that aggression in me." That is not true. First of all, you were born of a warrior. The Lord is a man of war. The Lord is a warrior, and when He comes back, He will come back as a warrior.

Some people have characteristics that make them a better warrior, but most people have to be trained to be a soldier. Women make the best soldiers. Look at the women who fought, for example, during the time of the Indians. When someone was caught, they were given over to the women for torture. Soldiers are made. They have to be trained and disciplined. I am more trained and focused today.

When children have to go to school, they are too immature to realize how valuable it is. Once they understand the value of what is being taught they will actually get something out of it.

If we were attacked today, you women would not run and hide. You would find out what you could do to help. You have a part to play. The women have as big a part as the men do in this last day. How humiliating it must be to Satan to be beaten by women. You have to apply yourself.

I fight very few battles for myself. Almost every battle I fight is for somebody else. I sow constantly. I lay hands on other people. I don't get sick. It is amazing how God protects me. I go eighteen to twenty hours a day, easily. Usually twelve of that is driving.

I pray for my spirit. I can go, because I pray out of the spirit and not out of the flesh. There are kids that have a hard time keeping up with me. I would rather burn out than rust out. I would rather keep on going.

After ministering one time in Florida, we left to go and eat before we had an appointment that we had to keep. A man from the meeting saw me as we were leaving the restaurant and asked me to pray for someone. I said, "Okay." After we prayed for them, he said, "I know someone else just down the road." I said, "Okay, one more." After that, he said, "I know a nursing home not even a mile from here," and I said, "Okay." How can I say no? What am I supposed to say? Am I supposed to say, "I am sorry? I am busy, just go die?" I can't do that.

The Secret to Constant Victory

I believe that when I lay hands on people, they will be well. I believe that, because in my spirit, that is what keeps me going, even when there is no success. I have a secret for you. In a war there are casualties. The hardest thing to do is to bury someone. We have buried a couple. It doesn't feel good. It hurts, and it makes me mad. People will die, but as time goes on, it is getting better and better. Less people are dying.

What are you going to do if that person does die? Are you going to quit? All of a sudden, this isn't true anymore, because that person died? Now, what do you do? Get back up, and keep on going. Go and pray for someone else, and prove that you believe the Word, now, more than ever. Prove that you want to do that more than anything else you can do.

The key is to keep on going and persevere. You keep on going. You keep pushing. You keep doing. Why? It is because that Book tells you to. That Bible is the only physical contact that we have with God. We have nothing else. There is no man's opinion, nor any other book that can prove contact with God.

You are in an army, now. You are being molded into the image and likeness of Jesus Christ. You are being conformed to his image. He is a warrior. A warrior can march to his death without opening his mouth. The last thing a warrior will do is open his mouth and say something that will discredit and show weakness to his kingdom. Jesus didn't do it, and we aren't going to do it.

If we go to our knees, it is to be in prayer and not in submission to some devilish tyrant somewhere. Are you going to bow your knees to sin? No. It is easy to beat sin. You are tempted by what you want to do. A man is tempted by his own lusts.

Satan doesn't tempt me to smoke or drink, because I have never done that. I hate it, as a matter of fact. He will put in front of you something that you like and that you have probably done before. Remember the last time you committed that sin? How did you feel immediately afterward? The next time you are tempted to sin, you will remember how you felt, and you will beat that every time, and your sinning days will be over. It works.

What is the key? What is the secret to victory? I just read it to you by George Patton. *"There is only attack and attack and attack some more."* The church, historically, has been in defensive mode. "If the devil will leave me alone, I will leave him alone. Maybe if I am quiet and camouflaged, he will go to my neighbor's house and won't come to mine." Even if he does go away, he will come back to you. You can't just sit back. You have to attack.

I am going to give you a martial arts analogy. If you are in a defensive mode and you are hit, it won't hurt, because there is no power behind the punch when you are backing up. The first thing you want to do is go on the offensive, and get the enemy on the defensive. Get the enemy against the ropes, and keep hitting him. If you hit him enough times, you will hurt him. Hit him everywhere, as often as you can, whether you hurt him or not. When you hit him enough times, you will get him on the run, so that he starts blocking and stops punching. You won't have to worry about getting hit anymore.

The Secret to Constant Victory

We live in the attack. As I said, I seldom have to pray for myself. I pray for someone else, and I keep doing something aggressive. Even if I am not fighting at the moment, I keep an aggressive attitude, so if the enemy shows up, he will see the snarl on my face, and say, "I don't want any of that."

According to General Patton, there are three keys to victory. They are speed, surprise and boldness. Get there quickly. The speed is the surprise aspect. That is the same thing William Tecumseh Sherman used in the Civil War. If you get there quickly, you will get there before the enemy gets there and gets set up.

"Well, that's good for you, because you travel and preach, but how do I apply it to my life? I get up and go to work every day. I haven't left my town in three years. How does this help me?" You are a part of the body of Christ. You are either in, or you are out. You are a cell in the body of Christ, and the Bible says that every joint fitly joined together supplies a part to the rest of the body. You may not be a missionary, but you can be here as support. I am not talking about money, although that is a part of it. You are behind the lines.

Do you realize that the Pentagon is behind the lines? It doesn't take a general to push the button. All it takes is the general to give the order, and those with no stripes all the way up to officers can push the button, and when they push that button, a city disappears.

You have time to do what you want to do. "How is your prayer life?" "I could pray more." "Why don't you?" "I don't have time." "Yes, you do. You have to make time. Take a nation and start praying for that nation." "Who am I? I am nobody." The Word is made up of a bunch of nobodies.

Who was Patton before he got into a war and proved himself? Who were any of those men? They were nothing. Who was Smith Wigglesworth, or John Lake, or any of those men? Had Smith Wigglesworth gone to school, he would have been voted most likely to fail. Smith Wigglesworth couldn't even read until his wife taught him at fifty years old, and yet, from that time on, after he got baptized in the Holy Ghost up until the time of his death, he shook the world. This was all because he decided to trust God. He said, "I would rather die believing than live doubting." People are still talking about him.

People say, "I wish I were Wigglesworth." Really? Then you would have the same battles he had. One of the battles he had was kidney stones, and he had them for years. When he would get through preaching, he would go home, soaked in blood.

He kicked a baby off the stage one time that was dying from disease. Someone caught it, and it was perfectly healed. He did some wild things, and if you are going to do things like that, it better be God. At the same time, he would stand for hours and pray for people, and when he went back to his room he would be soaked in blood because of the kidney stones.

We see the victories and the things that go on and the testimonies and their glory in life and the big names on the marquee, but we don't realize the battles they go through.

You might say that I haven't come very far, but if I was to stand up and say, "This morning, I ran a mile in only thirty eight minutes," you would say, "I could walk a mile faster than that." I would say, "I forgot to tell you. I was carrying three hundred pounds." "Oh, well, that is impressive."

It is not always the things you accomplish but the things you overcome. Right now, you may think you are getting beat, but God has you picked out to overcome and win. Do you know how you will lose? You will lose if you give up and quit. All you have to do is keep heading in the right direction.

A young man called to tell me that his mother-in-law was dying and had less than 24 hours left to live. He asked me if I would pray, and I said, "Yes, hand her the phone." I prayed for her and had her give him back the phone. I told him to stand and lay hands on her every time he was around her, and command life.

He called me back later and told me that there was no change. I said, "What do you mean there is no change?" He said, "There is no change." I said, "What did you tell me the first time?" He said, "That she was going to die in 24 hours." I said, "Then there has been a change, because it has been 36 hours, and she is still alive." Every day she lives, we prove the doctor and the devil a liar, and we win.

Every day is a victory. Every day that you get up and do it again is a victory. You are a soldier, and you are going to have to decide that you are going to be disciplined. You have to decide that you are going to do what this Book says, and you are going to keep plodding along. You may plod slowly, but keep moving.

Strength to Carry On

Have you ever seen a vulture land on something that is still moving? No, they wait until they are sure it is dead, and there is no movement. Why? It is because they are cowards. If you keep moving in the same direction, demons will leave you alone, because they don't like a fight. If you fall flat on your face, at least kick, or move your finger. Let these things know that you are not dead.

At least fall in the right direction. I don't care if you have to crawl there, at least head that direction, and keep moving. If you keep moving, it is not over until you say it is over and until you say, "I give up." Keep moving forward, because sometimes that is all you have going. I don't care how bad it is, keep going.

There have been times when it looked like all hell was breaking loose against us in the ministry and personally. There are times that I have gone off to meetings and preached and had miracles, and people had no idea what was going on at home and in the ministry. On the way to the meeting, I would pray, "God, get me through this day. I am going to keep on going and deal with tomorrow, tomorrow."

People are dying waiting for someone to get there. You can't back off. You can't stop. You have to keep moving forward. You have to develop an old fashioned grit. Get around some of the older, mature people. You will find out that the one thing you can learn from your elders is grit. Get stubborn.

"I hate to lose." Stand and keep on moving forward. Grit your teeth, and say, "No, bless God. If you are going to take me out, then you are going to have to hit a moving target. I don't care

The Secret to Constant Victory

how it feels, I am not going to give up, stop or quit." As long as you don't stop, you win. You need to realize how you are going to win and why you are going to win. Matthew 8:5-10 says,

> 5 And when Jesus was entered into Capernaum, there came unto him a centurion, beseeching him,
>
> 6 And saying, Lord, my servant lieth at home sick of the palsy, grievously tormented.
>
> 7 And Jesus saith unto him, I will come and heal him.
>
> 8 The centurion answered and said, Lord, I am not worthy that thou shouldest come under my roof: but speak the word only, and my servant shall be healed.
>
> 9 For I am a man under authority, having soldiers under me: and I say to this man, Go, and he goeth; and to another, Come, and he cometh; and to my servant, Do this, and he doeth it.
>
> 10 When Jesus heard it, he marveled, and said to them that followed, Verily I say unto you, I have not found so great faith, no, not in Israel.

How did this man have such great faith? He understood authority. Matthew 8:11-13 says,

> 11 And I say unto you, That many shall come from the east and west, and shall sit down with Abraham, and Isaac, and Jacob, in the kingdom of heaven.

12 But the children of the kingdom shall be cast out into outer darkness: there shall be weeping and gnashing of teeth.

13 And Jesus said unto the centurion, Go thy way; and as thou hast believed, so be it done unto thee. And his servant was healed in the selfsame hour.

Matthew 7:28-29 says,

28 And it came to pass, when Jesus had ended these sayings, the people were astonished at his doctrine:

29 For he taught them as one having authority, and not as the scribes.

That is the one thing you see over and over again in the life of Jesus. They kept saying, "He talks with authority. When He tells people to do something, they do it."

Mark 1:21-27 says,

21 And they went into Capernaum; and straightway on the Sabbath day he entered into the synagogue, and taught.

22 And they were astonished at His doctrine: for He taught them as one that had authority, and not as the scribes.

23 And there was in their synagogue a man with an unclean spirit; and he cried out,

24 Saying, Let us alone; what have we to do with thee, thou Jesus of Nazareth? Art thou come to destroy us? I know thee who thou art, the Holy One of God.

The Secret to Constant Victory

25 And Jesus rebuked him, saying, Hold thy peace, and come out of him.

26 And when the unclean spirit had torn him, and cried with a loud voice, he came out of him.

27 And they were all amazed, insomuch that they questioned among themselves, saying, What thing is this? What new doctrine is this? For with authority commandeth he even the unclean spirits, and they do obey him.

They were astonished at the fact that the demons listened to Him. They said, "This is really something. This man has some authority when even demons listen to Him." Mark 1:28-34 says,

28 And immediately his fame spread abroad throughout all the region round about Galilee.

29 And forthwith, when they were come out of the synagogue, they entered into the house of Simon and Andrew, with James and John.

30 But Simon's wife's mother lay sick of a fever, and anon they tell him of her.

31 And he came and took her by the hand, and lifted her up; and immediately the fever left her, and she ministered unto them.

32 And at even, when the sun did set, they brought unto him all that were diseased, and them that were possessed with devils.

33 And all the city was gathered together at the door.

34 And he healed many that were sick of divers diseases, and cast out many devils; and suffered not the devils to speak, because they knew him.

Mark 1:39-42 says,

39 And he preached in their synagogues throughout all Galilee, and cast out devils.

40 And there came a leper to him, beseeching him, and kneeling down to him, and saying unto him, If thou wilt, thou canst make me clean.

41 And Jesus, moved with compassion, put forth his hand, and touched him, and saith unto him, I will; be thou clean.

42 And as soon as he had spoken, immediately the leprosy departed from him, and he was cleansed.

Luke 10:16-19 says,

16 He that heareth you heareth me; and he that despiseth you despiseth me; and he that despiseth me despiseth him that sent me.

17 And the seventy returned again with joy, saying, Lord, even the devils are subject unto us through thy name.

18 And he said unto them, I beheld Satan as lightning fall from heaven.

> 19 Behold, I give unto you power to tread on serpents and scorpions, and over all the power of the enemy: and nothing shall by any means hurt you.

How can we quote that we have authority, and yet, we don't believe that nothing shall by any means hurt us? You have to start to walk in the fact that nothing shall by any means hurt you.

For you to walk in that, the first thing you have to kill is fear. The number one fear you have to break is the fear of man, because the fear of man will keep you from praying for people out loud and in public places like Wal-Mart.

Luke 10:20 says,

> 20 Notwithstanding in this rejoice not, that the spirits are subject unto you; but rather rejoice, because your names are written in heaven.

You have to break the fear of death, and you have to realize that nothing can touch you. Why? It is because if you rejoice in the demons being afraid of you, then that is all you have, but if you rejoice in the fact that your name is written in heaven, then the entire kingdom of God belongs to you, and you have access to everything He has.

Matthew 8:18 says,

> 18 And Jesus came and spake unto them, saying, All power is given unto me in heaven and in earth.

How much authority? All authority has been given to you both in heaven and in earth. That is a lot of authority.

Matthew 28:19 says,

> 19 Go ye therefore………

Is there anywhere that He doesn't have authority? He has it in heaven and in earth. Why? It is because He has all authority.

We have been given all authority in heaven and earth. In other words, "Nothing shall by any means hurt you." You are going to trample on serpents and scorpions. "I am giving you authority." What authority is He giving you? He is giving you the same authority He has. You operate in His authority.

We have been taught that we have delegated authority, but what we have is inherited authority. We are in Him. It is not your authority. You don't have a bit of authority. He gave you His authority, because He is in you. You have His authority to operate.

The centurion said, "I am a man under authority." When you are under authority and something goes wrong, you can say, "It's not my deal. It is his." You also know how much authority you have, because it is based on who gave it to you.

If the mayor gives you authority, you know you don't have authority outside the city limits, but if the governor gives you authority, then you have authority in the entire state but not outside the state. Why? It is because your authority is based on the person that gave you the authority.

The Secret to Constant Victory

If Jesus has all authority in heaven and earth, how much authority do you have? You have all authority over heaven and earth.

Galatians 4:1 says,

> 1 Now I say, That the heir, as long as he is a child, (which is you) differeth nothing from a servant, though he be lord of all;

The heir is lord of all. We know that Jesus is Lord of all, and because He gives you the same authority He has, that means you are also lord of all. We know that Jesus is King of kings and Lord of lords. We have been made kings and priests unto our God. We are the kings He is King over and the lords He is Lord over.

When you begin to act like a king and a lord over your area of influence, you will begin to speak with authority and take authority, and you will begin to walk in authority and demons will flee from you, and sickness will flee. It has nothing to do with anything except that Jesus lives in you. It does not have anything to do with you and how holy you are or how good you are.

The drawback to that is if you don't live holy, your conscience condemns you, and at that point you will be unable to pray with authority, because you will know you don't deserve it. I can tell you now, you don't deserve it, but when you sin, condemnation is there.

The Bible says, "If your heart condemns you, then you have no confidence towards God, and if you don't have confidence, you don't have faith, because faith is confidence."

Matthew 28:19-20 says,

> 19 Go ye therefore, and teach all nations, baptizing them in the name of the Father, and of the Son, and of the Holy Ghost:
>
> 20 Teaching them to observe all things whatsoever I have commanded you: and, lo, I am with you alway, even unto the end of the world. Amen.

Did He command us to heal the sick? Yes. We are supposed to teach all nations, and we can't teach them to do it if we can't do it ourselves.

That is why I can pray for you and lay hands on you, and you will be healed, because I too am a man under authority. I can say go, and the sickness will go. I can say come, and healing will come. Why? It is because I am under His authority, and Jesus did it, so I can do it. That is how it works. You are also under authority, and you can do the exact same thing.

What is authority? Authority is pre-permission. That is all it is. If someone gives you authority, they are giving you permission before hand to do something. You have authority to tread upon serpents and scorpions and over all the power of the enemy. You have authority to heal the sick. You have authority to cast out devils. If you have authority that means He gives you pre-permission to cast out devils and heal the sick.

You don't have to ask, "Can I heal this person? Can I cast out this devil?" Why? First of all, it is because it isn't you healing, it is Jesus in you, and He has given you pre-permission. You don't have to ask permission, because He has already given you pre-permission. Authority is just pre-permission.

If you go to a car dealership, and say, "I want to pay this amount down," he would say, "I don't have authority to make that deal. Let me talk to my boss." He is going to get permission. That's why he didn't have authority, because he didn't have pre-permission. Once he gets permission, he has authority to make the deal. What is he doing? He is getting pre-permission to make that deal.

You have pre-permission to heal the sick. You don't have to ask. You have pre-permission to cast out devils. You have pre-permission to pray for someone and expect them to get well. You have pre-permission to do whatever that Book tells you to do. We have pre-permission. Do you see what freedom there is in that?

I don't worry about missing it. "What if I set someone free that God didn't want free?" Do you know what you are actually saying? "What if I have more compassion than God does?" What do you think the odds are that you are going to have more compassion than God? Did you sacrifice your son on the cross to die for man? He has more invested in it than you do.

It is time for us to take part. He said, "The fig is ripe, the harvest is ready, but there are not enough laborers." Then He turned around, and commissioned seventy more in addition to the twelve. Did the harvest die? Is there no harvest today? The harvest is greater today, because there are more people living today than ever before. They said, "Lord, increase our faith."

He said, "If you had faith, you would speak to this tree, and it would die. You would do these things, and you would hear it come out of your mouth." Right after that He said, "Say not there is yet four months unto the harvest. Look, the harvest is ripe right now." In other words, don't wait.

You can't get ready to heal the sick and raise the dead. He made you ready when you were born again. It is not you raising the dead. It is the Spirit of your Father in you. Every dead person that has been raised so far, He did it. That is why the Bible says that the same Spirit that raised Jesus from the dead dwells in you.

We always emphasize that He will quicken our mortal body, but we ought to emphasize that the Spirit that raised Jesus from the dead dwells in you. That means the same Spirit that raised Jesus dwells in me and in you, which means every sick person that has ever been healed, the Spirit in me and in you has done it already.

"Well, I don't know what to do." Don't worry about it. He has been in this same situation every time. You can't make yourself ready. You will always fall short. You will always make a mistake, and that thing will ride you. He is ready. Get out of the way, and let Him do it. How do you get out of the way? You say what this Book says, and you do what this Book says, and you will know you are led by the Spirit of God.

Mortify the deeds of the flesh. When the flesh says, "Don't stick your hand out and heal that person. Do you want to look like a fool?" You need to say, "Yes, I need to. I am going to kill the flesh." When you do that, you know you are being led by the Spirit, and the Spirit in you will set that person free, and you will see God work through your hands.

What is authority? It is pre-permission. I am not saying God won't speak to you or lead you. I am saying, "If you don't feel it or sense it, do what the Book says. You already have permission."

This is a statement the Lord gave me: "You prove that you have great faith by handling specific situations with general orders." In this Book, it doesn't tell you to go to Wal-Mart at seven o'clock and pray for the lady in the red dress on aisle four. That is a specific situation. He can't give you specific situations in this Book. It would be impossible to write every situation for every person. He cannot do it. Stop expecting Him to. He gives you principles to operate by.

"Believers," which is you, "shall lay hands on the sick, and they shall recover." What are you going to do? "God, do you want me to pray for this person?" You just proved you don't have any faith, because a person with faith handles specific situations with general orders.

How many of you work for a company with specific instructions in an operations manual? They have you read what you are responsible for. The better the teacher, the more they operate by principles rather than by specifics. Jesus was the greatest Teacher. He gave us principles, and He expects us to operate in them at all times.

Anytime you see a specific, think of a general principle that it fits, and do it. When you do that, you prove that you trust God. This is the only contact you have with God in the physical realm. When you take this, you prove you believe what He said, instead of saying, "Give me a word, give me a confirmation, and give me a prophecy." He will do those things, but the more He gives you, the less faith you operate in. The greatest faith only has to be told once, and you have already been told.

STRENGTH TO CARRY ON
Messages to Strengthen Your Commitment

YOU HAVE A DESTINY

The first thing Paul said to Timothy was, "Teach the same Gospel that I (Paul) preached and the same Gospel that Jesus preached." In 2 Timothy 2:1-7, Paul was saying to Timothy:

1. Thou therefore, my son, be strong in the grace that is in Christ Jesus.

2. And the things that thou hast heard of me among many witnesses, the same commit thou to faithful men, who shall be able to teach others also.

3. Thou therefore endure hardness, as a good soldier of Jesus Christ.

4. No man that warreth entangleth himself with the affairs of this life; that he may please him who hath chosen him to be a soldier.

5. And if a man also strive for masteries, yet is he not crowned, except he strive lawfully.

6. The husbandman that laboureth must be first partaker of the fruits.

7. Consider what I say; and the Lord give thee understanding in all things.

We have to preach the Gospel of hope and of grace, but at the same time, we also have to preach the Gospel that says, "Take heed to yourselves." In other words, "Don't teach other things."

Paul mentions Timothy in the first verse, but the other men aren't important enough for him to mention. He told Timothy to pass this by saying, "You commit this Word to them." In 2 Timothy 2:2, it says,

> 2 And the things that thou hast heard of me among many witnesses, the same commit thou to faithful men, who shall be able to teach others also.

The word pass is actually a weak word compared to commit. He told Timothy, "You commit this to them." The word commit is the same word as commission. He told Timothy to commit to these men the responsibility of preaching this Gospel and sharing it with others.

He told Timothy to do the work of the evangelist. What stood out to me is that he didn't say who to pass it on to. He was saying, "Find some faithful men." In other words, it doesn't matter who preaches the Word of God, just make sure they are faithful men. Commit it to them, and let them pass it on.

Essentially, if we take this to be the Word of God and that this is for us, then we believe the Word. In 2 Timothy 2:15, Paul says,

> 15 Study to shew thyself approved unto God, a workman that needeth not to be ashamed, rightly dividing the word of truth.

If all of this is for us, then we have to realize that God, through Paul, was also telling us to take the Gospel, and commit it to faithful men and women, who will in turn, also pass it on. It is just like when Jesus said, "When you go out and make disciples, command them to observe all things I have commanded you."

One of the things He commanded them was to go out and make disciples and to pass it on to them, which means that when the disciples taught other people, they also had to command them to go out and teach others and make disciples. In other words, "Now, you teach other people, because that is part of the commandment." Jesus wanted this to be perpetual. If it goes in your ears, it should come out of your mouth.

I have a deep theology for you, "If you aren't doing it, then you aren't doing it." It's really simple. You can't say you are if you aren't. That is the deception.

James 1:22 says,

> 22 But be ye doers of the word, and not hearers only, deceiving your ownselves.

If you are a hearer and not a doer, you will deceive yourself, and the first deception is that you are a doer of the Word when all you are is a hearer. We have to realize that God wants us to be doers. Part of being a doer is to commit what we have heard.

One way to become totally confused is to sit down in front of your Christian television at eight o'clock in the morning and remain there until about noon, because you will hear one thing after the other; all different from the other.

I've had people come to me telling me that they are confused about things. When I asked them where they heard what they were confused about, they told me they were listening to

Christian television. I asked them if they wanted deliverance, and if they did, then they needed to turn off the television. That is the first step towards deliverance.

First take heed to what you hear. Next, take heed to your doctrine. Once you have this message and you know it's true, pass it to someone else. The next thing he told them to do was to commit it to faithful men who shall be able to teach others also. He is showing that he wants it to be perpetual.

Notice the next part in 2 Timothy 2:3,

> 3 Thou therefore endure hardness, as a good soldier of Jesus Christ.

"Thou therefore…" Why? It is because they have to be able to pass it on. Then it says, "…endure hardness." Part of the hardness he is talking about is trying to pass it on to people, especially with Timothy.

Paul told Timothy not to let anyone despise his youth. "Don't let anyone say that because you are young, they aren't going to listen to you." He was going to teach things to people who were older than he was. At the same time, they were going to be saying, "Who are you to teach us?"

Maybe chronologically he was younger, and maybe he was younger in Christ as well, but it is not the age that matters. It is the revelation, and the walking, and faithfulness to continue to walk in the Word of God that counts.

You Have A Destiny

We recognize elders, both age wise and as far as the Word goes, but the main thing I want to emphasize is this: Paul said to endure hardness. He even had some hardship.

That is one thing humans don't want to endure today. Our life is geared towards comfort and convenience. The main reason people have abortions is because of convenience. It is time to go back to principle.

If you want a message title, I would say, "It Is Time," because time is of the essence. We are at a crossroads right now in America and in Christianity. It is amazing. All these things like science, religion, economy, and national politics, are coming together and converging at one time.

We have to be awake. We can't sleep. We can't just say, "The Lord's will be done." We are to say that, and we are to do the will of the Lord. What am I saying? It is time. It is time to quit whining.

The Bible says, "Quit you like men." It is time to stand up and do the right thing. Choose the right thing. Go by principle and not by convenience. Stand up for a principle. You need to vote by principle. Go for what is right.

A true Christian will vote for what will benefit the majority. The whole of humanity is more important than any one person. It is time for you to be healed. It is time for you to quit waiting for healing and to be healed.

There was a time when God winked at sin. He held off. It isn't that they got by with it, but there was a purpose behind it. You are here at this time, in this place in history. You are not a mistake. God saw you. He knew you would be here. He knew what would take place.

I don't know how many times I have said that I would like to have been around during the days of Jesus or in Smith Wigglesworth's time or when John Lake was alive. It would be great to go to a Smith Wigglesworth meeting.

You have to be careful, because you can second guess God. I tell people in a joking fashion that I was born a hundred years too late. I should have been born during the circuit preacher's time, but at the same time, I know God put me at this time for a reason. God has a purpose. He has a plan. God said, "I know the thoughts and the plans I have of you; thoughts of good and not of evil."

We need to realize that God has a plan, and there is a time, and this is that time. You are a vapor, and then you are gone. I recently preached a message that has been with me for a while, because I couldn't get it to come out right. When it came out, it was, "Living a Life that Matters." This is a residue of that.

Most Christians live a life, so that when they are gone, the world can't tell the difference. "Yeah, but I am just one person. What am I going to do?" What if Martin Luther had said that? We would be in a different setting today. If Charles Parham had said that, everything would be different today. You are one person, but you have Christ in you, and you can make a difference. Now is the time.

It is time to stop living a life like one man said, "A life of quiet desperation." Stop living a life of quiet desperation. We are the overcoming, glorious, Church of God. That's who we are. We are in that body. He is in us. Christ in you is the hope of glory. Be blunt.

Colossians 1:27 says,

> 27 To whom God would make known what is the riches of the glory of this mystery among the Gentiles; which is Christ in you, the hope of glory.

We are soldiers. We are to do our job. It is amazing.

Look at God. When you aren't saved, He will woo you in and send people your way until you finally get in. It is like you are the only person on earth, and He sees it that way. He is working to get you saved.

God is a lot like a military recruiter. They will wine you and dine you and tell you what you want to hear, to get you to sign up. God doesn't wine you and dine you, but when you sign up and raise your right hand and make that oath, you are all that matters.

Once you make the oath, He sends you out there, and all of a sudden, you are expendable. When we die, we go to the Lord. What I am saying is, "We have to expend our life for others."

The entire thing is that you just have to learn to die. In the past, the big problem in the church was that we weren't dead enough. We tried to hold on to the church, or to God, with one hand and the world with the other. That is what creates that struggle and that turmoil.

Strength to Carry On

There was a man recently that was hiking and got caught under a boulder by one arm. He had a pocket knife and cut his arm off. I don't know how long I would have to be caught before I made the decision to do something like that. Could you imagine the turmoil he went through and the commitment he made once he did it? Once he did it, he was free.

Jesus said, "If your eye offends you, pluck it out. If your right hand offends you, cut it off." The problem is that we want everything we have. We don't want to lose anything. We don't want to pluck out our eye. Jesus said if we don't die, He can't have our lives. He said, "If you will lay down your life, I will give you my life."

There has to be that "laying down of life." There can't be resurrection without a death. Nobody wants to die, but without death, there is no resurrection. At some point you have to decide. I am going to die to everything I was; every part of me. I am going to lay down my life and pick up His.

I am not saying I have attained this, but I have learned this. Everything I have laid down, God has given back to me, so much so, that I promise you, not only do I not miss it, but I have learned to hate it.

I have realized how long that part of my life has kept me from walking in the fullness and the blessings of God. I stop and think, "Why was I so stupid? Why did I fight and struggle against God?"

If you won't lay your life down, with your goals, your agenda, your aspirations (which must change after you are saved), then what makes you think you are saved? If you lay down your life, then your life should cease looking like your life and begin to look like the life of Jesus. If you truly laid down your life, and picked up His, Jesus should be living through you. People should see more Jesus through you.

People should come to you, and say, "You are so different. You aren't like you used to be. I wanted to talk to you, but we just couldn't communicate." You should say back to them, "Praise God, that guy was no good. The only thing good in me is Jesus." To the degree that we let Him live His life through us, Christ is seen.

There will be a time in history when a people will "grow up into Him." Think about growing up into Him.

Ephesians 4:15 says,

> 15 But speaking the truth in love, may grow up into Him in all things, which is the head, even Christ:

You are going to change your heart. You are going to change your mind. You are going to change your actions. There will be some outward changes. You are not to be conformed to this world. Don't let the world squeeze you into its mold. Don't let it make you look like it.

Romans 12:2 says,

> 2 And be not conformed to this world: but be ye transformed by the renewing of your mind, that ye may prove what is that good, and acceptable, and perfect, will of God.

You are to be transformed by the renewing of your mind. That takes place by allowing what is on the inside to shine outward. Let Christ, Who is in you, be seen on the outside. We are to "grow up into Him in all things." You may say, "That is foreign to me. I am so far from that."

We are all so far from that. I dare say that any of us are truly faithful representatives of Christ. We are all at different levels of stages and growths. We are all moving forward and growing, and that is the key.

I heard a guy talking about diet, and he made this statement: "It is not perfection. It is progress." The Bible does say to be perfect and mature as God is perfect and mature. He says to quit sinning, so you are to get out of sin. "Sin shouldn't even be named among you." It is like the old saying, "I may not be what I want to be, but thank God I am not what I was." There is progress.

You may not be perfect yet, but don't keep saying, "I am not perfect." Every time you say that, you move farther away from perfect. Quit saying that, and quit thinking that way, because if you continue to look at yourself that way, then you will never make progress toward perfect.

The Bible says that we grow up in Christ. By growing in grace and learning all these things, you are dying a piece at a time, on a daily basis, and replacing that with Christ's life.

Ephesians 4:15 says,

> 15 But speaking the truth in love, may grow up into Him in all things, which is the head, even Christ:

You Have A Destiny

In 2 Peter 3:18, it says,

> 18 But grow in grace, and in the knowledge of our Lord and Saviour Jesus Christ. To Him be glory both now and for ever. Amen.

Most people are waiting for something that never comes. The reason they wait for it is because they don't know what it is going to be like when it comes. If you have never seen it, how will you know what it looks like when it comes? It could pass you by, and you wouldn't even know it.

"How will I know when I see it? I'm not perfect. How will I know if I don't know what it looks like?" The main thing is that you are making progress. You don't just say, "I messed up today." Get up. Dust yourself off. Go to God, and then go again. Keep moving forward.

Are you waiting for God to do that thing? If you are born again, then that has already happened. People are waiting for something that has already happened. You are in Christ, waiting for something else to happen that has already happened and is in the past.

That is like someone saying, "I am going to give you a house," and then you go to a lot, and it is in stacks of brick, wood and materials. Did they give you a house? Sure, they did, but you have to put it together. You have to work with what you have. If you know what you are doing, it will look really good.

Our problem is that we keep waiting for God to show up with a complete house. We are all part of God's house, and He is building us step by step, brick by brick, every day. Some of us are pretty rough, and He has to pick us up, clean us off, and get us right, and He does that bit by bit every day.

We are raw materials, but we have to walk that out. Christ dwells in us. We put Him in a straight jacket and won't let Him out. He wants to be Jesus like He always was, but we won't let Him out.

I told some people the other day to picture this: you are walking down the street one day, just minding your own business, and all of a sudden something happens, and in the blink of an eye, you are standing before the throne of God.

God says, "I brought you here, because I have a plan. I have a mission for you to go on. Will you do it?" You say, "Sure, Lord. I will do whatever you say." "It won't be what you are used to." "God, you are God, and I will do whatever you want."

God says, "Here is the plan. The devil is roaming around all over the earth, and I want to get Jesus back in there, but I don't want him to see Jesus come back in, so I have to sneak Him in. Have you ever heard of a Trojan horse? I want you to be a Trojan horse.

Here is what I want you to do. You are going to stay here with me. I am going to take your spirit out of your body and send your body back to the earth as a Trojan horse for Jesus' Spirit to be in." You say, "Okay, whatever you say, Lord. I get to stay in heaven." It sounds good. He says, "You sit over here, and watch."

All of a sudden, you are back on the earth. You get to watch your body walk over the earth, but come Monday morning, you don't go back to your job. You could go there, but Jesus is on a mission. He has an agenda. You think, "Wait. Take my body to my job," then you think, "That isn't me, so it doesn't matter."

You see your body walking along, and all a sudden, you see Jesus stop, reach over and touch a sick person, and they are healed. Word spreads, because they don't see Jesus, they see you. You go on, and keep doing it.

What is Jesus doing? He's being Jesus, but in your body. If it is the same Jesus, we ought to be doing the same thing. How do we know we have the same Jesus if He is not doing the same thing? You think, "That is really far fetched." It's not that far fetched. The Bible says, "It is no longer I that live, but Christ that lives in me." This is found in Galatians 2:20-21,

> 20 I am crucified with Christ: nevertheless I live; yet not I, but Christ liveth in me: and the life which I now live in the flesh I live by the faith of the Son of God, who loved me, and gave Himself for me.
>
> 21 I do not frustrate the grace of God: for if righteousness come by the law, then Christ is dead in vain.

Colossians 1:27 says,

> 27 To whom God would make known what is the riches of the glory of this mystery among the Gentiles; which is Christ in you, the hope of glory:

It's not Christ in you that is your hope of getting glory. That's not what it is about. It is that Christ in you is glory's hope.

Heaven and glory have a hope, and that is Christ living in you and being able to live through you.

We are to be seated with Him in heavenly places. Isn't that why Jesus left here? Isn't that amazing? It is a science fiction type story, and it is totally scriptural. Is that violating Scripture? No. You ask, "What about the 'zipping out' part?" Look in the Bible, and you will find that in there too. That is where it speaks of the rapture.

The difference is that now, you can actually picture what takes place. There has been an exchange. People say, "I could never heal the sick." You are right. You can't, but Christ in you can. Well, "I don't know what I am doing." That's good, because Christ in you does. He's been there. He's seen it, and He has done it.

I was in Georgia a while back, and we were in a mall exchanging clothes and shopping. I brought a book to read while I was waiting for my wife and daughter to finish their shopping. I wasn't spiritual. I was complaining and grumbling about wasting time in the mall when I could be at home working.

While I was standing there, a woman and her daughter, who was about 16, walked up. I had been praying that weird things would happen. I didn't want to see people die. I wanted to see people healed. I had been praying, "God, do the unusual. I am ready. Here I am. Use me."

While I was standing there, I literally could feel liquid pouring out of my side like a tube toward them. I thought, "Where is that going?" I looked over, and I saw the girl, and it was going toward that girl. God was having compassion.

I was working with it. I was pushing and believing at the same time. In about five minutes, she said, "I feel a lot better." I didn't lay hands on her. I thought, "Wow! That's really neat."

I wanted to walk over to her, and say, "The anointing of God healed you," but it was too late to do it then. That would be like being a prophet September twelfth. Don't come tell me what September eleventh was. Come to me on September tenth, and tell me what's going to happen the next day, and then, you are a prophet.

The next day I was sitting at home writing and watching a video that someone had sent me from Africa, about healing. The video was playing, but I really wasn't paying attention to it when, all of a sudden, I felt the same thing that I felt at the mall, but it was going forward.

I looked up, and right then a healing was taking place. There was a cancer the size of a head of lettuce on this boy. It just fell off. This tape was over a year old. The boy had been healed when I got the tape.

I was confused, and I thought, "That is weird, God. What is going on? I felt it, but it happened a year ago." God said, "What happens when you remember when you were in a life threatening situation, and then you start talking about it?" I said, "My breathing gets shallow, and my heart starts beating faster. My blood pressure goes up. The more detailed I tell it, the more I relive it, and the more physical effects take place, even though I am not in danger." After I said all of that, God said, "What is going on is that the Holy Spirit was remembering healing that boy. He was reliving it."

At that same time, I remembered that verse, "The same Spirit that raised Christ from the dead dwells in you. He will quicken your mortal bodies." I had always preached the last part of that verse, "He will quicken your mortal bodies," but that was the first time I had ever had a divine commentary on the first part of that verse.

Do you realize that the Spirit that dwells in you has performed every healing that has ever taken place? Every healing and every person that has been raised from the dead that you have heard about dwells in me and dwells in you, and He did it. I can't do it, but He can. I am ready. Why? It is because He is ready.

That changed my life. All of a sudden, I was ready. I couldn't pray enough. I couldn't fast enough. Does He have to pray and fast to get ready? No. Then I don't have to do it. I can't do enough good things to get ready. I am ready.

I am not saying don't pray and fast, but don't use it as some kind of arm twisting for God to be ready. I am ready. Every healing that has ever taken place, He did it.

Matthew 10:1 says,

> 1 And when he had called unto him his twelve disciples, he gave them power against unclean spirits, to cast them out, and to heal all manner of sickness and all manner of disease.

We say, with no problem, that the disciples healed the sick. We can say that about them, and it is safe, but if I walk in, and say, "I have been out healing the sick," religion immediately says, "You can't say that. Who do you think you are?"

When they act like that, I am going to say, "Oh, I am sorry. I thought you were more mature. Let me talk to you on your level. Christ was healing the sick through me. He and I were out together. I laid hands on the sick, and He healed them. Is that better?" When we are mature enough, we don't have to say it that way, because we know that no person can heal the sick.

When we blow up like that, it is because we are too immature, and we automatically think someone is trying to get in pride. When we think that someone is in pride, it is because we are in pride, and we judge them according to our own hearts. We need to let people be who they are. We don't have a problem saying, "Jesus healed the sick," or "The disciples healed the sick."

How many of you believe in Jesus? How many of you believe in the name of Jesus and have faith in the name of Jesus? We all agree that we have faith in the name of Jesus, because without it, we aren't saved.

Strength to Carry On

There are two verses every Christian should know. They are: John 3:16 and Acts 3:16.

John 3:16,

> 16 For God so loved the world, that he gave his only begotten Son, that whosoever believeth in him should not perish, but have everlasting life.

Acts 3:16,

> 16 And his name through faith in his name hath made this man strong, whom ye see and know: yea, the faith which is by him hath given him this perfect soundness in the presence of you all.

Acts 3:1-4 says,

> 1 Now Peter and John went up together into the temple at the hour of prayer, being the ninth hour.
>
> 2 And a certain man lame from his mother's womb was carried, whom they laid daily at the gate of the temple which is called Beautiful, to ask alms of them that entered into the temple;
>
> 3 Who seeing Peter and John about to go into the temple asked an alms.
>
> 4 And Peter, fastening his eyes upon him with John, said, Look on us.

Stop right there. Wait a minute. "Peter, you are in pride, brother. You know they can't look on you. You aren't supposed to say that." "Oh, that's right. Let's just look to the Lord." That is not what Peter said, is it? He said, "Look on us." It goes on to say,

> 5 And he gave heed unto them, expecting to receive something of them.
>
> 6 Then Peter said, Silver and gold have I none; but such as I have give I thee.

Most of us could still say that along with Peter. We are equal with Peter. "Silver and gold have I none." Has Peter said anything yet that we can't say so far? No. What does Peter say that they have? Let's allow Peter to answer:

> 6 In the name of Jesus Christ of Nazareth rise up and walk.

First of all, he obviously had the name of Jesus. In verse 7 it says,

> 7 And he took him by the right hand, and lifted him up…

Apparently, the man didn't get up quickly enough for Peter, so instead of waiting for him to get up, Peter reached down and grabbed him and pulled him up by his right hand. Obviously his right leg wasn't working yet, so he lifted him up. He didn't help the man stand. He lifted him. The rest of verse 7 says,

> 7 …and immediately his feet and ankle bones received strength.

Do you realize the man's feet and ankles were not healed until Peter lifted him up? There is a Scripture in 1 Corinthians 12 that talks about miracles. What we want is the gift of miracles, and yet, there is no such thing. There is a gift of the working of miracles. That is what Peter was doing. He was using his gift of the working of miracles. The gift of miracles is really the gift of faith. The gift of faith is you standing there, and saying, "Watch," and God doing it.

In 1 Corinthians 12:28-31, it says,

> 28 And God hath set some in the church, first apostles, secondarily prophets, thirdly teachers, after that miracles, then gifts of healings, helps, governments, diversities of tongues.
>
> 29 Are all apostles? are all prophets? are all teachers? are all workers of miracles?
>
> 30 Have all the gifts of healing? do all speak with tongues? do all interpret?
>
> 31 But covet earnestly the best gifts: and yet shew I unto you a more excellent way.

The gift of miracles, the gift of faith, operates when you say, "Watch," and God does it through you. There is a working, which is why we don't see miracles in church, because nobody wants to work them. It requires faith.

God wants you to step out on the line. He put His name out there. He is stepping out, and He wants you to step out with Him. It doesn't take faith to say, "Watch, and see what God is going to do." It takes faith to say, "Watch," and lift that person up.

Acts 3:8-9 says,

> 8 And he leaping up stood, and walked, and entered with them into the temple, walking, and leaping, and praising God.
>
> 9 And all the people saw him walking and praising God:

The man wasn't even praising God until he was healed. When people get healed, it brings glory to God. The man was not sitting there everyday bringing praise to God as a cripple. It even goes farther than that in verse 10. Watch this:

> 10 And they knew that it was he which sat for alms at the Beautiful gate of the temple: and they were filled with wonder and amazement at that which had happened unto him.

The amazing thing is, the Scripture says, "These signs shall follow believers." Where do you put signs? You put them where people will see them. The signs we put out for everyone to see are healing of the sick, speaking in tongues, and casting out devils.

In 1 Corinthians 14:22 it says,

> 22 Wherefore tongues are for a sign, not to them that believe, but to them that believe not: but prophesying serveth not for them that believe not, but for them which believe.

"Tongues are a sign; not for the believer, but for the unbeliever." Then why do we only speak in tongues in church? We are all believers. If we are going to have signs, it will draw attention to us, and everyone will look on us, which is why they are called signs. The last part of verse ten in Acts 3 says,

> 10 ...and they were filled with wonder and amazement at that which had happened unto him.

"They were filled with wonder and amazement." That is what signs do. We need to start doing signs out in the public where people can see them. There is nothing in here that says this man was godly at all. It says he sat by the gate where all the money was.

Any homeless person can sit at the front door of the church. As a matter of fact, that would be a good place to go, because of the hearts of the people that go there. That man got healed, because a godly person walked past him.

Continuing in Acts 3:11-12,

> 11 And as the lame man which was healed held Peter and John, all the people ran together unto them in the porch that is called Solomon's, greatly wondering.
>
> 12 And when Peter saw it, he answered unto the people, Ye men of Israel, why marvel ye at this? or why look ye so earnestly on us, as though by our own power or holiness we had made this man to walk?

In other words, Peter said, "I didn't do this in my own power. I am not holy enough to do this." There are two reasons people use as excuses not to heal the sick. "I don't have any power, and I don't live holy enough." Peter just said, "It isn't my power, and I don't live holy enough." Why aren't you healing the sick? Forget your excuses; you don't have them anymore. Acts 3:13 says,

> 13 The God of Abraham, and of Isaac, and of Jacob, the God of our fathers, hath glorified his Son Jesus; whom ye delivered up, and denied him in the presence of Pilate, when he was determined to let him go.

By the unction of the Spirit, God considered that the man's healing glorified Jesus. That is why he was healed. God was glorifying Jesus.

God was not vindicating that man's holiness. He was not saying that the man was holy. He was not saying he was right, or that this man's doctrine was right, or that his life was right. He was not saying that. He was saying, "My Son is going to be glorified. Watch how I am going to do it." It says in verses 14-16,

> 14 But ye denied the Holy One and the Just, and desired a murderer to be granted unto you;
>
> 15 And killed the Prince of life, whom God hath raised from the dead; whereof we are witnesses.
>
> 16 And His name through faith in His name hath made this man strong, whom ye see and know…

What made this man strong? God glorified His Son, so God did it. Peter said it, too. "What I have, I am going to give you, in the Name," so it was in the Name. It says, "His Name through faith in His Name." Back up. Has Peter said anything that you couldn't say? No.

You can say all of the things Peter said. "Silver and gold have I none." "What I have I give you." "I give you the name of Jesus." Do you have the name of Jesus? I could take out the name Peter, and replace it with your name. It would be the same thing. It is simple. The last part of verse 16 says,

> 16 ...yea, the faith which is by Him hath given him this perfect soundness in the presence of you all.

Peter had this faith, which was "by Him." In other words, "It was through faith in His Name." Do you want to know the secret of miracles? The people asked what they could do in John 6:28,

> 28 Then said they unto Him, What shall we do, that we might work the works of God?

Did Jesus say for you to fast and pray or for you to be good enough, long enough? He didn't say that, did He? What did He say?

> 29 Jesus answered and said unto them, This is the work of God, that ye believe on Him whom He hath sent.

You believe on Him, and you have the Name. You thought you could hide behind something. You can't hide behind anything. The Word of God is like a hammer, and it will blast all the rocks you try to hide behind. Everything you need is right here. "In the name of Jesus, be healed. In the name of Jesus, rise up and walk."

Have you ever noticed that Jesus was a man of few words? He always talked in few words. "Be healed." "Rise and walk." "I will." We pray shotgun prayers, hoping that one of our prayers is going to help. We pray with one eye open, watching to see what happens, but change doesn't occur until you quit praying and asking God; start using what you have been given. It is that simple.

I went out to eat with a family that said they had questions about healing, but there wasn't one question. They just wanted to pin me down. The woman kept saying, "Healing is so complicated." I just wanted to say, "Stop saying that healing is complicated. It is not complicated."

If you say things like that, all you will do is confuse the people. It is simple, because if you apply enough power to something, your problem will be gone. That is all healing is. Keep applying more power of God, which is faith in the name of Jesus.

We try to have faith in our faith. Don't have faith in your faith. Have faith in God. God is your God. Your faith will fail. Peter's faith failed for a while.

We need to realize that we don't need to read this Bible backwards, but that is what everyone tries to do. Jesus said, "If you have faith the size of a grain of mustard seed, you can move this mountain." We try to make it so hard. We say, "If I have faith the size of this mountain, I can move this mustard seed."

If you walked up to a friend of yours, and said, "Are you going to the store with me?" and he said, "Yes, I will go with you." "Are you sure you are going with me? I am trying to believe that you are going to go with me." That person will hear you calling them a liar. We don't do that do we? "God, I am trying to believe. Just give me a sign."

Do you know that by questioning God, we are saying, "God you are such a liar. I just can't believe you. I am trying. Just give me a sign. Do something to show me, and I will believe you." You have already received every sign you are going to get. In Matthew 16:4, Jesus said,

> 4 A wicked and adulterous generation seeketh after a sign…

John 20:29 says,

> 29 Jesus saith unto him, Thomas, because thou hast seen me, thou hast believed: blessed are they that have not seen, and yet have believed.

Jesus said, "A wicked and adulterous generation seeks a sign," and "You are more blessed, because you believe without seeing." We have got to believe. We have got to do this. It is amazing.

Jesus said in Luke 4:18,

> 18 The Spirit of the Lord is upon me, because he hath anointed me to preach the gospel to the poor; he hath sent me to heal the brokenhearted, to preach deliverance to the captives, and recovering of sight to the blind, to set at liberty them that are bruised,

"The Spirit of the Lord is upon me, because He hath anointed me to preach the Gospel to the poor," but we turn it around, and say, "I am anointed, because the Spirit of the Lord is upon me." You probably think, what is the difference? Didn't He say the same thing twice? No. Jesus didn't say, "I am anointed, because the Spirit is upon me." Jesus said, "The Spirit is upon me, because I am anointed."

When you are anointed, it draws the Spirit of God, and when the Spirit of God comes on you, you can do all things through Christ who strengthens you. That strengthening is the Spirit. When you say, "I have the Spirit of God," then you are strengthened. You shall receive power after the Holy Ghost, the Spirit of God, has come upon you.

You are anointed, and that draws Him, so you can do these things. The difference is that many people think that you are anointed from time to time, when the Spirit shows up, but Jesus said, "Because I am anointed (all of the time), I have the Spirit (all of the time)." Like Jesus, we have the Spirit all of the time.

It is time. What is going to change? I promise you that God is not going to change. You can say, "I need more power." "All power is given unto you in heaven and earth, now, you go." Every excuse you give Him for not doing it, He will have a Scripture. Why? It is because, "Forever My Word is settled in heaven."

He is not going to change one bit for you and me. It is settled. It is set. Whenever we line up with Him, things happen. He is waiting on us. It is time.

In 2 Timothy 2:15, it says,

15 Study to show thyself approved unto God, a workman that needeth not to be ashamed, rightly dividing the word of truth.

The word "study" here is the Greek word *spoudazō* and is pronounced spoo-dad'-zo. It means *make effort, be earnest: be diligent, endeavor, labor, study*. You are to *be diligent*. That means, be faithful, pray, seek after God, and pursue God; and thereby by *being diligent*, a doer of the work of God. If you are a doer of the Word, you are blessed, because you will be a doer of the work.

A workman is not someone who just sits; that is a hearer. A doer is a workman. Hearers of the Word and not doers of the Word need to be ashamed. I am saying, "Quit being a hearer, and be a doer, and you won't have to be ashamed. There is no shame in Him. You will never be put to shame. Your enemies will be put to shame."

Rise up! It is time! Today is the day of salvation! The word *salvation* means *healing and deliverance*. Do you need healing or deliverance? Today is the day! Have you been saved? Today is the day for salvation! You need fullness! Today is the day!

JGLM Trademarked Names

All derivatives of JGLM names are Copyrighted trademarks:

Divine Healing Technician(s)
John G. Lake Ministries
John G. Lake Healing Rooms
John G. Lake's Divine Healing Institute
Dominion Life International Apostolic Church
Dominion Bible Institute

All derivatives of these names are Copyrighted trademarks and may not be used without the express written permission of:

John G. Lake Ministries
P. O. Box 742947
Dallas, Texas 75374
www.jglm.org

Please advise JGLM if you come into contact with anyone using the following names without authorized permission:

John G. Lake Ministries
John G. Lake's Divine Healing Institute
John G. Lake Healing Rooms
Divine Healing Technicians Certified
DHT

Appendix A: Historical Information

1. The information presented in this book is for historical purposes only. References to people, organizations, professions, etc., are presented for the sole purpose of giving an accurate overall understanding of the prevailing viewpoints of particular groups, religions, denominations, and movements of the time periods referred to in the seminar.

2. Each reader is expected and required to make personal comparisons and decide for themselves which viewpoints to accept and endorse.

3. The material presented and its successful application is predicated upon the viewpoints of those during the time periods in which they lived.

4. Curry R. Blake and John G. Lake Ministries are in no way responsible or liable for the successful application of the material or for future re-presentation of the materials presented in this book.

Appendix B: Practices Concerning Medicine Or Medical Treatment

1. All information presented is not to be construed as advice or instruction in activities or practices concerning medicine or medical treatment.

2. The author of this book is not in any way a trained medical or psychological professional.

3. Any ministry services are being rendered from a position of compassion and mercy and are not to be construed as medical treatments or as substitutions for medical treatments.

4. No one can present themselves or anyone under their guardianship for ministry, without relinquishing and waiving all legal recourse that would or might be the end state of such person and/or anyone they present for ministry.

5. Anyone using this material cannot hold JGLM liable or responsible for their personal practice of ministry.

Appendix C: Rules For Reproduction Of JGLM Materials

1. The physical material in this book is and shall remain the property of the presenter and the JGLM organization they represent. All material in this book shall belong to the author.

2. No reproduction of the material in this book is allowed without express written permission from the author of this book.

3. Any material and/or information in this book or gained during the seminar or from audio/video material from the host organization, if presented to others at any time, shall be presented in its entirety as it is presented in this seminar, without change, adaptation, omission or addition.

4. Prior to the presentation of this material to any other persons, groups, and/or organizations, reader will contact and inform the presenting organization of personal intentions in writing. If told not to present the information, such person(s) are not to present it.

5. In the event said person is given permission to present information, they are to provide the host organization with an audio/video recording (in its entirety) of the material presented.

APPENDIX D : NON-MEDICAL ADVICE

1. The information presented in this book is in no way intended as advice or instruction concerning the use of medicine, medical treatment, or the avoidance thereof.

2. Each person is responsible to investigate all methods of remedy they are contemplating.

3. No one has a right or responsibility to make your decision except you.

4. Any reference to medicine or medical treatment is solely for historical or informational purposes.